"**NOMAD** spiritually *sizzles* with heart-felt hone and sorrows, Brilliant"

Kary Oberbrunner, author of *ELIXIR PROJECT, Your Secret Name, The Deeper Path*, and *Day Job to Dream Job*

"Through prose, poetry, scripture and reflection, Timothy Carroll artfully weaves life's journey of yearning and failure, discouragement and hope to new life in Christ. **NOMAD** is honest, pensive and candid about Timothy's own struggles, questions and doubts about himself, the church and religious pretenders. It will challenge those who feel like aimless nomads yearning to discover the true captain of their lives."

Rev. Bill Lyle, Peace Church, Pickerington, Ohio.

"I have known Timothy only for a few of his 40 plus years. They were busy years discovering how far on this path we had to go. The unexpected journey that you are about to embark on is a true journey. It is a raw journey. I found myself staring at the page very often asking, 'Did he just say that?', as I read page after page. His poetry tells of the spiritual journey like no sermon can, like no spiritual leadership or self-help book can. As I read **NOMAD**, I found myself wanting him to get to the good news but I found myself completely identifying with the bad news, or the real news. But as I moved from page to page it was so imperceptible I almost did not recognize it—the Good News of what God did for me and in me was rising like the morning sun in each and every page—and what I thought was bad news, what my soul screamed out wanting to make into somebodies fault, was all the while God orchestrating this beautiful life that He has been waiting for me to surrender to all along. **NOMAD** is a must read for anyone, most of all the weary spiritual warrior".

Dan Glover, Lead Pastor Tipp City United Methodist Church; President-*Deepening Your Effectiveness .Org*, Co-Author of *Deepening Your Effectiveness*

Having worked with Timothy Carroll on several ministry projects over the years. I was both amazed and humbled by the birth of **NOMAD**. Timothy's creativity and writing talent come to life speaking raw spiritual truths to the reader.

Marty McCabe, Business Owner, Youth Pastor, and Founder and President of *Illumination Festival*

NOMAD

ESCAPE THE DARKNESS RELEASE YOUR BAGGAGE AND EMBRACE A NEW LIFE OF SPIRITUAL FUSION

TIMOTHY W. CARROLL

To all of you who's "ripples" have blessed and guided my nomadic journey. There are far too many to even begin to mention…. Thank you, and God bless.

A very special thanks to my amazing bride, Tina. The fact that you love me the way you do is proof that there is a God.

And to my Savior. Thank you Jesus for your amazing free grace, and your boundless love. You never stopped chasing me.

CONTENTS

Foreword xi

Introduction xv

1 Ripples 1

2 To Kill, Steal, and Destroy 28

3 Stumbling and Bumbling 47

4 Obscure Baggage 54

5 Corporate Craftiness 70

6 Birthing Pains 87

7 Growing Pains 102

8 Aged Humility 121

9 Journey's End 132

10 Salt Air 142

Acknowledgements 153

About the Author 155

"The flowers have all faded

The grass no longer green

A dusty haze chokes the breath

That fireball towering above is laughing down on me

Solitary I stand"

FOREWORD

It was the summer of 2009 and my back was up against the wall. My wife Kim and I had sold our house and had to be out in 30 days. When Kim first approached me about selling our house, I thought it was a bad idea at the time. However, we prayed on it, and to my surprise, I felt like the Lord was indeed telling me to sell our home; so much so that we met with our pastor, whom I deeply respected as a wise man of God, to get his opinion. Pastor Dan put a nice spin on it for me. A "safety net", if you will. Pastor Dan told me to be obedient and just put the house up for sale. It may not sell anyway, and if it didn't, I was still being obedient. The housing market at the time was horrible. We had a huge, stately old home and I was sure I was safe and it would not sell. I was wrong.

So we had 30 days to get out. We had lived in this house for 20 years with our 8 children. We were now down to two teenage kids, Tim and Jess. Our temporary plan (that turned out to be five years) was to move into the one bedroom apartment above my chiropractic office. Between the apartment, my office and our basement, there would be plenty of room I reasoned. Again, I was wrong. We had accumulated massive amounts of God knows what. Still, I did not panic, because I was in one

Cincinnati Reds and Bengals, and was even a team physician one night for the Cleveland Browns. I say this not to brag but, to say how blessed I am, and to point out that Timothy Carroll is as great as any person I have ever met. He is a true auteur and one of the few people that I know that has followed his calling without any concern for money or prestige. The greatest compliment that I can pay him in regards to **NOMAD** is this; once I asked Timothy if he would read his stuff to our youth group. We had a large youth group that was very active and very sociable. I think initially it put the fear of God into him. To put himself out there like that, show his insecurities, reveal his writings, especially to teenagers was quite frightening. If you have ever worked with youth you know that you could blow up a skyscraper with dynamite with fireworks going off and they would be bored. On the nights Timothy read his stuff, you could hear a pin drop. It was truly amazing.

So, read **NOMAD**. Read it for enjoyment. Read it to learn. Review the questions and it will change you. Share it and you will share yourself. And while you are reading **NOMAD** you won't have to go through your skull alone.

Dr. Patrick Harless, Chiropractor, Videographer, Author, Youth Director

INTRODUCTION

Many people have been deceived by "the church". Many of us were told that when we accepted Christ, "our worries, our problems, and our fears would go away". A half-truth is still a lie. I bought into that lie. I believed the lie.

It is one thing to claim Jesus Christ as your savior; to call yourself a Christian. It is a completely different thing to *know* the Christ.

What am I talking about? God has no desire to be a part of my life. God insists on being that which my life is all about.

If I could use only one word to describe how I visualize what my relationship with God should look like it would be *fusion*.

Fusion: the act or process of fusing or melting together; union. (Dictionary.com).

Think of it like this; in one cup you have very cold iced tea. In the second cup you have steaming hot tea. Now add a teaspoon of sugar to the ice cold tea and stir briskly. The tea is now semi-sweet. However, due to the very cold liquid, the sugar and liquid do not chemically bond. Much of the sugar drifts to the bottom of the cup. Now, add a teaspoon of regular sugar to the hot tea and stir briskly. In this case a chemical reaction takes place between the hot liquid and the sugar. They fuse together, becoming one, hence a *new* substance has been created.

This fusion of my life with the Creator of the universe is a life-long process. The key component in my walk is when I begin to understand and to embrace this concept of *"Spiritual Fusion"*.

Much of the writing in this book may seem dark. Instead, I would encourage the reader to simply see it as brutal honesty. Much of the writing represents a very lost and hurting soul screaming out for answers where there seemed to be none. I believed in the One True Christ and accepted Him as my Savior, my forgiver of sins. However, I simply did not *know* Him, or had forgotten that which I already knew.

It is my hope and my prayer, that you, the reader, will find hope and encouragement from these pages. Sometimes when life is at its darkest hour, we are not only seeking answers, but we also somehow need to know that we are not alone in what we are feeling. Somehow, if we hear or read of someone else's struggles, it can give us hope. We are reminded that others have fears, others battle depression, anxiety, addictions, etc. We are reminded, that a very real part of the human experience is in battling the darkness that so deeply pervades each life.

I have included relevant scripture at the end of each poem. This is designed to help you on your journey as you seek out ultimate truth and wisdom. Likewise, I have included a *Spiritual Fusion Assessment* at the end of each chapter for the purpose of challenging you, the reader, as you reflect on your personal growth into Spiritual Fusion with your Creator.

Remember, no matter how you *feel*, whether it be your darkest hour, or the most wonderful moment in your life, God is unchanging. His love for you is unconditional. He loves you the same, regardless of how you *feel*.

CHAPTER ONE
RIPPLES

We must all start somewhere right? What is it that shapes our lives, forms who we are and who we become? Is it our experience, our environment? Is it our genetics? How does intelligent design factor in?

As an example, I have agonized with anxiety ever since I was a small boy. I have dealt with this affliction my entire life. What one does with these afflictions is what ultimately determines both one's own future, as well as countless other lives.

Each choice is a ripple in time. It could be said that every choice one makes does indeed ultimately eternally effect the Universe as a whole. This I believe is intended by intelligent design.

However, we all come into this world with no previous experience, unlearned, with no prior source of reference. Then, in a blur, one's life begins and it ends.

What do each of us do with the ripples formed by others? The ripples formed by other's choices constantly bombard us. Then you in return, make decisions that send out ripples into the Universe, in turn affecting countless other lives. On and on and on it goes. A ceaseless, unfathomable number of ripples forming and reforming, never ending.

All of this begs the question, "How do I handle this constant bombardment of ripples from humanity?

My perspective and interpretation of these ripples will determine the direction of my life. Will I be controlled by these ripples? Will I learn self-control and wisdom, becoming uneasily swayed? Will I be teachable?

TIMOTHY W. CARROLL

139:13-18 (NLT) *"You made all the delicate, inner parts body and knit me together in my mother's womb. Thank or making me so wonderfully complex! Your workmanship is elous–how well I know it. You watched me as I was being d in utter seclusion, as I was woven together in the dark of omb. You saw me before I was born. Every day of my life was led in your book. Every moment was laid out before a single ad passed. How precious are your thoughts about me, O God. cannot be numbered! I can't even count them; they outnumber rains of sand! And when I wake up, you are still with me!"*

SIXTEEN

My Dad and I,
We really are two very differe[nt]
He is so serious
Such a perfectionist
Me, I am a dreamer.
He sees me as lazy
We mix like oil and wa[ter]
Never getting along
Never seeing eye to ey[e]
I've stopped trying to pleas[e]
Why attempt the imposs[ible]
I can do nothing righ[t]
All is negative
I'm certain he no longer lik[es]
I know he loves me,
He would die for me without [hesitation]
As I would for him
Nevertheless, he does not like [me]
He seems burned out
Tired of being my fathe[r]
I'm certain that he prays for the da[y]
This hurts so deeply.

I pray that someday
We will sit down togeth[er]
Sit as two grown men
That we would sit and talk like[men]
But as long as I live her[e]
There will only be strife
There is no getting along anywh[ere]

ANXIETY

Time to go
Got to get moving
Time to get up
Really should be going
But oh, that constriction in my chest...
Sitting in this house
Free from danger
Stuck right here
On this couch
Looking out the window
Checking things out
Should be getting up
Should get going
I don't know...
What's the big hurry?
What's the big rush?
Not like anyone will miss me much
Sit a little longer
Let it linger
No hurries here
Ponder what's left of my sanity
Drink a little wine,
Then go face humanity

Proverbs 12:25 (NLT) *"Worry weighs a person down; an encouraging word cheers a person up."*

Philippians 4:6-7 (NLT) *"Don't worry about anything; instead, pray about everything. Tell God what you need, and thank him for all he has done. Then you will experience God's peace, which exceeds anything we can understand. His peace will guard your hearts and minds as you live in Christ Jesus.*

Matthew 6:25-34 (NLT) *"That is why I tell you not to worry about everyday life-whether you have enough food and drink, or enough clothes to wear. Isn't life more than food, and your body more than clothing? Look at the birds. They don't plant or harvest or store food in barns, for your heavenly Father feeds them. And aren't you far more valuable to him than they are? Can all your worries add a single moment to your life? And why worry about your clothing? Look at the lilies of the field and how they grow. They don't work or make their clothing, yet Solomon in all his glory was not dressed as beautifully as they are. And if God cares so wonderfully for wildflowers that are here today and thrown into the fire tomorrow, he will certainly care for you. Why do you have so little faith? So don't worry about these things, saying, "What will we eat? What will we drink? What will we wear? These things dominate the thoughts of unbelievers, but your heavenly Father already knows all your needs. Seek the Kingdom of God above all else, and live righteously, and he will give you everything you need. So don't worry about tomorrow, for tomorrow will bring its own worries.*

SOLITARY

The flowers have all faded
The grass no longer green
A dusty haze chokes the breath
That fireball towering above is laughing down on me
Solitary I stand
They have all scurried off
Seeking comfort and safety
In what they know.
My hunger is ravenous
Always seeking,
Not yet finding
I see their cruel smiles
Tell me, who is the fool?
Seeking purpose
Questioning the unquestionable
Pushing for answers
In the end, a solitary man…

Romans 8:38-39 (NLT) *"And I am convinced that nothing can ever separate us from God's love. Neither death nor life, neither angels nor demons, neither our fears for today nor our worries about tomorrow-not even the powers of hell can separate us from God's love. No power in the sky above or in the earth below-indeed, nothing in all creation will ever be able to separate us from the love of God that is revealed in Christ Jesus our Lord."*

Psalm 142:4-5 (NLT) *"I look for someone to come and help me, but no one gives me a passing thought! No one will help me; no one cares a bit what happens to me. Then I pray to you, O Lord. I say, "You are my place of refuge. You are all I really want in life."*

Psalm 32:7 (NLT) *"For you are my hiding place; you protect me from trouble. You surround me with songs of victory."*

COLD EASTERN WIND

Tonight that cold wind is blowing in from the East
Just can't seem to get warm
I'm hungry for the feast
Empty inside, nothing fills me up
Sitting here alone
This cold empty house, cold as stone

I hear that wind blowing
The windows they are rattling
My mind wonders back…
To times gone by

Where did it all go?
How did I arrive at this place?
So many dreams, so many hopes.
Now it's all changed
And that Cold Eastern wind blows…

I sit and I wonder
Where did it all go so wrong…?
Have I always been so lost…?
Tonight I am broken and very alone
And still… that cold Eastern wind, it blows

I've journeyed far
I've seen and done a lot
I've been blessed by so many
And hurt by countless others
I have loved deeply,
And I have lost much
And tonight I am all alone
And still that cold Eastern wind blows

I've let countless down along the way
I've been selfish and foolish many would say
Like a raging bull in a china shop
I've arrived at this spot
But this bull's been clipped
And now here I sit
And I can hear that cold Eastern wind blowing

---

1 John 1:8-10 (NLT) *"If we claim we have no sin, we are only fooling ourselves and not living in the truth. But if we confess our sins to him, he is faithful and just to forgive us our sins and to cleanse us from all wickedness. If we claim we have not sinned, we are calling God a liar and showing that his word has no place in our hearts."*

Psalm 34:5 (NLT) *"Those who look to him for help will be radiant with joy; no shadow of shame will darken their faces."*

Psalm 31:16-17 (NLT) *"Let your favor shine on your servant. In your unfailing love rescue me. Don't let me be disgraced, O Lord, for I call out to you for help…"*

Ecclesiastes 7:20 (NLT) *"Not a single person on earth is always good and never sins."*

WAKE

It's raining outside tonight,
So dark and cold
Feeling all alone…
Just don't feel right
Restless, tired
Feel so weary tonight

Missing you hurts so much
Can't be selfish though,
I *want* to be strong
Tired of doing what is wrong

So much pain inside this man
So much destruction I've left in my wake
I hurt the ones that I held close
Want to make it all alright…
If I can…

These demons from my past
They won't let me go
The prison walls that I've built
Hold those demons close

On my knees now,
Begging for your help
Wanting a new life
Looking for hope

Pry my fingers from these prison bars
Save me from my own destruction
Don't want to go out like this
Heal me from these scars

Missing you hurts so much
Can't be selfish though
I *have* to be strong
I'm tired of doing what is wrong

So much pain inside this man
So much destruction I've left in my wake
I hurt the ones that I held close
Want to make it all alright…
If I can…

Acts of the Apostles 9:19-21 (NLT) *"… Saul stayed with the believers in Damascus for a few days. And immediately he began preaching about Jesus in the synagogues, saying, "He is indeed the son of God!" All who heard him were amazed. "Isn't this the same man who caused such devastation among Jesus' followers in Jerusalem?" they asked. "And didn't he come here to arrest them and take them in chains to the leading priests?"*

Psalm 23:4 (NLT) *"Even when I walk through the darkest valley, I will not be afraid, for you are close beside me. Your rod and your staff protect and comfort me."*

2 Corinthians 4:17-18 (NLT) *"For our present troubles are small and won't last very long. Yet they produce for us a glory that vastly outweighs them and will last forever! So we don't look at the troubles we can see now; rather, we fix our gaze on things that cannot be seen. For the things we see now will soon be gone, but the things we cannot see will last forever."*

TORN

I feel so torn tonight
My soul is twisted
My mind is tormented
I am worn tonight

I cry out to you
I read the red letters,
I think of you
I talk to you
I listen to you

Sometimes I hear you

Then my Self cries out

Of course I must answer my Self.

Now I am shamed
You sit quietly
I cry
Once again, I cry out to you,
"When will it ever end?
This vicious behavior."

I am torn tonight

Romans 7:21-25 (NLT) *"I have discovered this principle of life-that when I want to do what is right, I inevitably do what is wrong. I love God's law with all my heart. But there is another power within me that is at war with my mind. This power makes me a slave to the sin that is still within me. Oh, what a miserable*

person I am! Who will free me from this life that is dominated by sin and death? Thank God! The answer is in Jesus Christ our Lord. So you see how it is: In my mind I really want to obey God's law, but because of my sinful nature I am a slave to sin."

Jeremiah 17:9 (NLT) *"The human heart is the most deceitful of all things, and desperately wicked. Who really knows how bad it is?"*

Galatians 5:16-17 (NLT) *"So I say, let the Holy Spirit guide your lives. Then you won't be doing what your sinful nature craves. The sinful nature wants to do evil, which is just the opposite of what the Spirit wants. And Spirit gives us desires that are the opposite of what the sinful nature desires. These two forces are constantly fighting each other, so you are not free to carry out your good intentions."*

CATARACTS

When exactly did it all go so gray?
The colors, they all eventually seem to fade…
Like a mutt with cataracts;
Black and white and blurred.
I'm not sorry
I'm certainly not living in regret.
But I didn't see it coming,
All those bright colors simply gone.
Looking ahead,
Look at that gray sunset off in the West
Death, life…
It's all the same.
I blinked and the color had gone.
They say that change is good…
Funny, like you have a say.
Laugh, cry…
It's all the same.

At one time the colors, they were blinding
No, not now,
Now it's very black and white, and very very blurred.

Hebrews 13:14 (NLT) *"For this world is not our permanent home; we are looking forward to a home yet to come."*

Colossians 3:2-3 (NLT) *"Think about the things of Heaven, not the things of earth. For you died to this life, and your real life is hidden with Christ in God."*

JUST AROUND THAT BEND

Living around that corner
What's around that bend?
Not right here,
Not right now.
I keep living the what *could* be
The what *will* be

Can't seem to quit living for what *might* be
I'm not living in the here and now.

Stuck thinking about
What's around the corner?
What's around that bend?

So disgusted with what's inside
I want it all for you

Too much of this heart belongs to me
You still do not own.

Living around the corner
What's around the bend?
Not right here,
Not right now.

Crush me into dust if you must
Break me down
Rattle my cage
If you must.

This strong willed man
He must finally die

Let your light
Blind this darkness
To set things right
If that's what it takes
Living around that corner
What's around that bend?
Not right here,
Not right now.

I keep living in what *could* be,
What *will* be.
Can't seem to quit living for what *might* be
I'm not living in the here and now.
No, I'm not living in the *now*.

I'm stuck thinking about
What's around the corner?
What's around that bend?

Philippians 4:11-12 (NLT) *"… for I have learned how to be content with whatever I have. I know how to live on almost nothing or with everything. I have learned the secret of living in every situation, whether it is a full stomach or empty, with plenty or little."*

1 Timothy 6:6-8 (NLT) *"Yet true godliness with contentment is itself great wealth. After all, we brought nothing with us when we came into the world, and can't take anything with us when we leave it. So if we have enough food and clothing, let us be content."*

SHE MUST ASK HIM WHY

Just as she must breath to stay alive
She must ask him why
She must ask him why
She doesn't have a choice
She can't let it go
She must ask him why
She must ask him why

Two hearts that grapple in the night
He simply doesn't want a fight
But she must ask him why
She has to ask him why

She lays there in anguish
Lays there in pain
She can't be content
Things simply aren't right
She must ask him why
He lays dazed and perplexed
What is it that he's done?
What is it that he's done?

On and on and on it plays
Two hearts that grapple in the night
He's too tired to keep up this fight.

Quietly he fades
Into his work he must go
In his work he is right
In his work there is no fight

Just as she must breath to stay alive
She must ask him why

> She must ask him why
> She does not have a choice
> She cannot let it go
> She must ask him why
> She must ask him why

Proverbs 5:18-19 (NLT) *"Let your wife be a fountain of blessing for you. Rejoice in the wife of your youth. She is a loving deer, a graceful doe. Let her breasts satisfy you always. May you always be captivated by her love".*

Genesis 2:18 (NLT) *"Then the Lord God said, "It is not good for the man to be alone. I will make a helper who is just right for him."*

1Peter 3:7 (NLT) *"In the same way, you husbands must give honor to your wives. Treat your wife with understanding as you live together. She may be weaker than you are, but is your equal partner in god's gift of new life. Treat her as you should so your prayers will not be hindered".*

Proverbs 18:22 (NLT) *"The man who finds a wife finds treasure, and he receives favor from the Lord".*

Proverbs 31:10 (NLT) *"Who can find a virtuous and capable wife? She is more precious than rubies".*

Proverbs 31:26 (NLT) *"When she speaks, her words are wise, and she gives instructions with kindness".*

1Corinthians 13:4-7 (NLT) *"Love is patient and kind. Love is not jealous or boastful or proud or rude. It does not demand its own way. It is not irritable, and it keeps no record of being wronged. It does not rejoice about injustice but rejoices whenever the truth wins out. Love never gives up, never loses faith, is always hopeful, and endures through every circumstance".*

EVER LEFT YOUR LOVER

Have you ever left your lover?
Have you ever just walked away?
Have you ever just had enough of the big play?
Just turned your head and walked away?
Dying on the inside
None of you left to give
Just got to break away
Just got to do this thing
Have you ever left your lover?
Just throwing in the ring
Have you ever just walked away?
Turned and walked away from that life
Nothing left to say,
Just walk away
Drying up on the inside
Already feeling dead
Guilt and shame raging inside
Have you ever just walked away?
No room to dream,
No room left to live,
So much hurt,
So much pain.
Have you ever just walked away?
Living with the guilt feels so much better now,
Living with her,
I was all alone.
Drying up on the inside,
Dying a slothful death.
Have you ever just walked away?
Have you ever left your lover?
Have you ever just walked away?
Have you ever just had enough of the big play?
Just turned your head and walked away?

Proverbs 21:19 (NLT) *"It's better to live alone in the desert than with a quarrelsome, complaining wife."*

Proverbs 27:15-16 (NLT) *"A quarrelsome wife is as annoying as constant dripping on a rainy day. Stopping her complaints is like trying to stop the wind or trying to hold something with greased hands."*

Proverbs 12:4 (NLT) *"A worthy wife is a crown for her husband, but a disgraceful woman is like cancer in his bones."*

Proverbs 28:13 (NLT) *"People who conceal their sins will not prosper, but if they confess and turn from them, they will receive mercy."*

SMILING STRONG

When I look back,
I am shamed...
The carnage and brokenness
Still visible in my wake.
When I look her way,
She's still smiling strong...
Her life,
It just seems to be slowly moving on.
This albatross that I drag along,
The guilt, as lead dangling from a chain
Affixed to my neck.
Blinded by all my own wrong,
Clumsily, I bumble on.
When I look her way,
She's still smiling strong.
She doesn't seem all caught up
In all that I've done wrong.
She keeps moving forward
Seeming to find her way.
So I stand here with a choice this day...
I lift up my head
Trying to be strong
Learning how to just move on
Praying for the day
When I can smile strong.
This life is so ironic,
So afraid to be all alone...
The world is so vast,
It's easy to find myself feeling
As though I am last...
But when I look back,
She's still smiling so very strong...

Philippians 3:13-14 (NLT) *"No, dear brothers and sisters, I have not achieved it, but I focus on this one thing: Forgetting the past and looking forward to what lies ahead, I press on to reach the end of the race and receive the heavenly prize for which God, through Christ Jesus, is calling us."*

Psalms 32:8 (NLT) *"The Lord says, 'I will guide you along the best pathway for your life. I will advise you and watch over you'."*

Jeremiah 21:11 (NLT) *"For I know the plans I have for you, says the Lord. They are plans for good and not for disaster, to give you a future and a hope."*

CROWDED CAFÉ

Sitting in this crowded café tonight
Feeling all alone
Sarcasm…
It reigns in my heart
I can feel it in my bones
On this cold dark winter night
I know this isn't right
I just don't care tonight

The singer, he's on that stage
He's singing one of those sad lonely melodies
And on this cold dark winter night
This sadness feels so very right

My spirit is so critical
I just don't seem to care
I know it isn't right
But that is where I am
On this cold dark night

Right here, right now,
On this cold dark winter night

What's wrong with this man?
So broken I've become
Why do I feel so dark?
Deep within
On this cold dark winter night

Right here, right now

Slip away…
Don't want to feel

Not tonight
No… not on this cold dark night.

Just slip away
Into myself
On this cold winter night

Right here, right now

The singer
He keeps singing those sad tunes
I'm drinking in all of his words
They just feed the sadness

Sadness is what I am
It's what I've become
It's where I want to be…

Right here, right now
On this cold dark winter night

I'm choking on the good spirit
That consumes this place tonight
People smiling, people laughing…
It all feels so surreal
I can't help but judge them
On this cold dark winter night

They laugh in folly
Living for the moment
Never thinking of tomorrow

Who am I to judge?

Right here, right now…

Gotta get out
Choking on the humanity
Choking on all of the eyes
Choking on the folly that surrounds me.

It smothers me
On this cold dark winter night

Right here, right now…

Ephesians 4:31-32 (NLT) *"Get rid of all bitterness, rage, anger, harsh words, and slander, as well as all types of evil behavior. Instead, be kind to each other, tenderhearted, forgiving one another, just as God through Christ has forgiven you."*

Proverbs 10:12 (NLT) *"Hatred stirs up quarrels, but love makes up for all offenses."*

Acts of the Apostles 8:23 (NLT) *"…for I can see that you are full of bitter jealousy and are held captive by sin."*

John 16:33 (NLT) *"I have told you all this so that you may have peace in me. Here on earth you will have many trials and sorrows. But take heart, because I have overcome the world."*

SPIRITUAL FUSION ASSESSMENT

Okay, it is now time to get out your journal and reflect. It is time to be brutally honest with yourself.

1. Make a list of negative behaviors and habits that you have acquired throughout your life from the "ripple affect".
2. Circle the emotions that have caused you to struggle the most throughout your life.
    a. Anxiety/Fear
    b. Worry
    c. Loneliness
    d. Bitterness
    e. Anger
    f. Pride
    g. Shame
    h. Unworthiness
    i. Self-Pity
3. Now, from your choices above; reflect on the circumstances that tend to provoke these emotions. What is the root cause of these emotions? Instead of pretending that these very real struggles do not exist, it is now time to face them head on. Acknowledge these negative feelings that are causing you to feel stuck in life.
4. To begin the healing process you must begin to daily meditate/pray, read, exercise. Simply walking 30 minutes a day can do wonders for the mind, body, and spirit.
5. Consciously seek out a (same gender) godly friend or mentor. Someone you can discuss your fears and struggles with.
6. Daily journal your struggles and your victories.
7. Meditate on Psalms 91

Psalms 91 (NLT) "Those who live in the shelter of the Most High will find rest in the shadow of the Almighty. This I declare about the Lord: He alone is my refuge, my place of safety; he is my God, and I trust him. For he will rescue you from every trap and protect you from deadly disease. He will cover you with his feathers. He will shelter you with his wings. His faithful promises are your armor and protection. Do not be afraid of the terrors of the night, nor the arrow that flies in the day. Do not dread the disease that stalks in darkness, nor the disaster that strikes at midday. Though a thousand fall at your side, though ten thousand are dying around you, these evils will not touch you. Just open your eyes, and see how the wicked are punished.

If you make the Lord your refuge, if you make the Most High your shelter, no evil will conquer you; no plague will come near your home. For he will order his angels to protect you wherever you go. They will hold you up with their hands so you won't even hurt your foot on a stone. You will trample upon lions and cobras; you will crush fierce lions and serpents under your feet!

The Lord says, "I will rescue those who love me. I will protect those who trust in my name. When they call on me, I will answer; I will be with them in trouble. I will rescue and honor them. I will reward them with a long life and give them my salvation."

CHAPTER TWO
TO KILL, STEAL, AND DESTROY

We all struggle to some degree or another. Struggling is part of the human condition. If you're not encountering struggles in your life, then you have no pulse.

How many of our struggles are actually self-imposed? If we are willing to be honest with ourselves, much of the pain that we experience is a result of our own selfish, self-indulgent choices and indecisions. Very often this seems to lead many of us down a path of unhealthy behaviors and addictions.

By our very nature, we are very selfish, carnal, fallen creatures. Why? I am a sinner. I was born with a sinful, i.e. selfish, nature.

The Book of Genesis tells the story of the fall of man. When Adam and Eve first walked the Earth they were without sin. Then, their curious minds got the best of them. The serpent lied to Eve; he convinced her that she was being lied to by God. He convinced her that if she wanted something, regardless of what God said, she should take it. Eve took what she wanted and shared with her husband, Adam. Then sin entered the world. Now they knew good from evil, and now all of their offspring would be born into this world with a fallen sinful nature.

Satan desires to kill, steal and destroy. That is his passion, his purpose. In no way am I suggesting that as a Christ follower you need to fear Satan. However, it is imperative that you understand how very real he is. Satan wants nothing more than to destroy you. His strongest weapon is to convince you that he is not real.

So I claim that Christ is my Lord. I acknowledge that Satan is a very real enemy. This brings us to our next point; not only asking forgiveness, but *repenting* of my sin.

Asking God to forgive me of my sins is in essence, asking God to pardon and to forget my sin. This enables me to avoid eternal separation from God. When I come to God through Christ and ask forgiveness, he freely forgives me. This is grace.

To come to God through Christ and *repent* of my sin is a much more profound action than to simply ask for *forgiveness*. To *repent* indicates a change of heart, to have deep remorse for my sinful behavior. Beyond simply asking to be *forgiven*, I now desire to change my ways. I desire to stop doing what it is I am *repenting* of.

The next step in this process of growth is to *own* it. Like Michael Jackson's hit song, "Man in the Mirror", it's time to take a good long look in the mirror. If you think that your life is a train wreck, or it is headed in that direction, then be honest with yourself about how you have ended up where you are. If you simply blame other people and situations for the dark place that you find yourself in, then you will remain imprisoned, frozen in misery.

My old sinful nature, which I refer to as "The Old Man", is very real. When darkness pervades my life, when I am feeling overwhelmed by life, The Old Man is very near. I can hear his haunting voice, calling to me. I find that when I am in a place in my life where I am seeking God out regularly, such as daily quiet time with him. Listening to him, spending quality time reading and studying the Bible, this is when The Old Man is muffled.

When I am seeking out Spiritual Fusion with my creator that is when I have hope. That is when I am able to experience peace. This is when I find rest.

HE APPROACHES

He approaches me
Like cold sharpened steel approaching a welcoming wrist

His voice like silk
He whispers…

"It is so very good"

He sighs

He crouches… and waits,
Patiently he waits

I contemplate this thing
This thing that lays before me

It seems so warm,
So comforting,
So inviting.

I sigh…

I hear his sighs…
It would be so enjoyable
So satisfying…

In his crouched position he smiles…
It is a cold unfriendly smile
Yet it draws me ever closer.

Closer to this thing before me

He is the cat
I have become his mouse

He whispers faintly in my ear
His voice ever so sensual

"This is what you need
This is what you want
Take it, it is yours"

My heart is pounding
My soul shutters
Sweat runs
My conscience numbs…

I concede

I have embraced it

I hear his shrill laughter
His mouth is gaping with it
He throws back his head

He roars

Like a mighty lion
He roars with delight

His voice is no longer as silk,
But mean, cold;
Like the piercing high notes dashing from a cello

'You are a fool, a weakling,
Your God is weak,
Weak like you"

"Crawl now to your pathetic Savior and repent to him
Then come back to me
As you know you will
I will be waiting"

Again, he laughs

Once again
I am defeated

By my own carnality
I have been defeated.

I fall to my knees,
I weep.

Freely he welcomes me
Into his bosom I collapse.

This vicious cycle must stop
It must end now.

I scream out,
"I am sorry my Lord!"

He holds me

Then,
Gently, but firmly, He pushes me back
He exposes his scared palms
I am reminded
Though I am fallen
It has all been swept clean.

This thing however,
This carnality within

> Like a malignant cancer
> It will endure…
>
> Endure it will, until eternity I do enter…

Ezekiel 28:12-19 (NLT) (The story of Satan's origins) *"…You were the model of perfection, full of wisdom and exquisite in beauty. You were in Eden, the garden of God. Your clothing was adorned with every precious stone – red carnelian, pale-green peridot, white moonstone, blue-green beryl, onyx, green jasper, blue lapis lazuli, turquoise, and emerald – all beautifully crafted for you and set in the finest gold. They were given to you on the day you were created. I ordained and anointed you as the mighty angelic guardian. You had access to the holy mountain of God and walked among the stones of fire.*

You were blameless in all you did from the day you were created until the day evil was found in you. Your rich commerce led you to violence, and you sinned. So I banished you in disgrace from the mountain of God. I expelled you, O mighty guardian, from your place among the stones of fire. Your heart was filled with pride because of all your beauty. Your wisdom was corrupted by your love of splendor. So I threw you to the ground and exposed you to the curious gaze of kings. You defiled your sanctuaries with your many sins and your dishonest trade. So I brought fire out from within you, and it consumed you. I reduced you to ashes on the ground in the sight of all who were watching. All who knew you are appalled at your fate. You have come to a terrible end, and you will exist no more".

Isaiah 14:12-15 (NLT) *"How you are fallen from heaven, O shining star, son of the morning! You have been thrown down to the earth, you who destroyed the nations of the world. For you said to yourself, 'I will ascend to heaven and set my throne above God's stars. I will preside on the mountain of the gods far away in the* *north. I will climb to the highest heavens and be like the Most High.' Instead, you will be brought down to the place of the dead, down to its lowest depths."*

John 8:44 (NLT) *"…He was a murderer from the beginning. He has always hated the truth, because there is no truth in him. When he lies, it is consistent with his character; for he is a liar and the father of lies."*

1 Peter 5:8-9 (NLT) *"Stay alert! Watch out for your great enemy, the devil. He prowls around like a roaring lion, looking for someone to devour. Stand firm against him, and be strong in your faith."*

TRAPPED

Merlot and a fine cigar
Melancholy
My life is eating away
Dwelling in my self-made prison
A prison cluttered with rash self-indulgent choices
I am trapped;
Trapped like a rat in a cage…

Psalms 40:1-2 (NLT) *"I waited patiently for the Lord to help me, and he turned to me and heard my cry. He lifted me out of the pit of despair, out of the mud and the mire. He set my feet on solid ground and steadied me as I walked along."*

Ecclesiastes 2:1-2 (NLT) *"I said to myself, 'Come on, let's try pleasure. Let's look for the 'good things' in life.' But I found that this, too, was meaningless. So I said, 'Laughter is silly. What good does it do to seek pleasure?"*

James 4:3 (NLT) *"And even when you ask, you don't get it because your motives are all wrong – you want only what will give you pleasure."*

OIL AND STEEL

On the razors edge he sits
Face wet with tears
Lacking capacity to provide
Half a man he's become

He is broken
All seems obscured
Irrational fears
They claw at his brain
Clarity has evacuated
Hope is but a faint reflection

His left hand clutches the pistol
Reluctantly his trembling hand rises
The 9mm is like lead
Ever so slowly to the chin

He can smell the pistol now
The oil...
The steel...

Ever so slowly the barrel
It slides between his lips
He can taste it now.
The Oil...
The Steel...

He hears his children laughing as they play
A shudder courses thru his spine
New tears flood...

His extremities become lifeless
The heavy steel falls to the floor

> Head bent
> Failure, despair
> Darkness pervades
>
> Defeated
> Sobbing he sits,
> On the razors edge, he sits…

Romans 8:32 (NLT) *"Since he did not spare even his own Son but gave him up for us all, won't he also give us everything else?"*

Deuteronomy 30:19-20a (NLT) *"Today I have given you the choice between life and death, between blessings and curses. Now I call on heaven and earth to witness the choice you make. Oh, that you would choose life, so that you and your descendants might live! You can make this choice by loving the Lord your God, obeying him, and committing yourself firmly to him. This is the key to your life."*

Romans 8:38-39 (NLT) *"And I am convinced that nothing can ever separate us from God's love. Neither death nor life, neither angels nor demons, neither our fears for today nor our worries about tomorrow – not even the powers of hell can separate us from God's love. No power in the sky above or in the earth below – indeed, nothing in all creation will ever be able to separate us from the love of God that is revealed in Christ Jesus our Lord."*

OLD MAN WITHIN

Once my former self…
He still dwells within
His appetite is insatiable
If he is not screaming to be set free,
He is moaning…

It never ends
He moans to be fed,
He begs that we feast,
That we may feed this carnal flesh.

Once upon a time he was king
He ruled this flesh of mine
High upon his throne of filth
He did rule.

However, no longer
He has been exposed

He lays naked
He lays in a cold damp and darkened place.
A place deep within me,
A place that I wish did not exist…
Nevertheless it does.

This is the reality that I must endure
Endure until my soul is released from this shell.

This shell which houses the very prison
That houses that which tortures my very soul.

1 John 4:4 (NLT) *"But you belong to God, my dear children. You have already won a victory over those people, because the Spirit who lives in you is greater than the spirit who lives in the world."*

2 Corinthians (NLT) *"This means that anyone who belongs to Christ has become a new person. The old life is gone; a new life has begun!"*

Colossians 3:10 (NLT) *"Put on your new nature, and be renewed as you learn to know your Creator and become like him."*

WHISPER

Whisper ever so gently in my ear
Please tell me all that I want to hear
Make it sweet,
Make it bright,
I'll just pretend that it's all alright.

I do want to hear it,
I will wait and listen
For in my ear
Your voice it does indeed glisten.

Though you be rotten through and through,
Still I am entranced,
I am enthralled with you.
And so I sit here waiting…
Just waiting to hear from you.

Psalm 119:27-29 (NLT) *"Help me understand the meaning of your commandments, and I will meditate on your wonderful deeds. I weep with sorrow; encourage me by your word. Keep me from lying to myself; give me the privilege of knowing your instructions."*

Galatians 5:19-21, 24 (NLT) *"When you follow the desires of your sinful nature, the results are very clear: sexual immorality, impurity, lustful pleasures, idolatry, sorcery, hostility, quarreling, jealousy, outbursts of anger, selfish ambition, dissention, division, envy, drunkenness, wild parties, and other sins like these. Let me tell you again, as I have before, that anyone living that sort of life will not inherit the Kingdom of God. Those who belong to Christ Jesus have nailed the passions and desires of their sinful nature to his cross and crucified them there."*

I AM HIS

Here I sit
I am broken and defeated
My face, wet with tears
Tears of pain
Pain that I have caused
So much darkness
Can't even see the Son
Hope, it is fading
My purpose here seems done
I sob,
And into the darkness I cry
Fear, it strangles my very soul
The light has gone out
He and his,
They surround me
Like famished hyenas they stalk
I hear their shrill icy laughter
Closer they come
Circle me they continue
One last cry to the Son
I bellow out
Then, He comes
Swiftly, stealthily, He comes
He and His slash and cut
The enemy and his, they cower
Into the darkness they vanish
Limp, exhausted I now am
Into His arms once again I collapse
The light is blinding
His perfect nature restores

Sob, I continue
Broken before Him
And I am reminded
That I am His

Psalm 3:3-4 (NLT) *"But you, O Lord, are a shield around me; you are my glory, the one who holds my head high. I cried out to the Lord, and he answered me from his holy mountain."*

Ephesians 6:11-12 (NLT) *"Put on all of God's armor so that you will be able to stand firm against all strategies of the devil. For we are not fighting against flesh – and – blood enemies, but against evil rulers and authorities of the unseen world, against mighty powers in this dark world, and against evil spirits in the heavenly places."*

LIE

Do you hear that whisper?
That whisper in your ear

Telling you to look
Just one more time

Do you hear that whisper?
That whisper in your ear

Telling you to cheat,
Telling you to lie,
Telling you that you won't die!

Do you hear that whisper?
That whisper in your ear

Well that whisper's just a lie!

Do you hear that whisper?
That whisper in your ear

Telling you to take a toke,
To take another drink,
Telling you that your life is just one big joke!

Do you hear that whisper?
That whisper in your ear

Close your ears to this world,
The world that is all around you,

> Now listen to the Christ
> He's the only answer
> He's the only way
>
> Do you hear that whisper?
> That whisper in your ear

John 15:19 (NLT) *"The world would love you as one of its own if you belonged to it, but you are no longer part of the world. I chose you to come out of the world, so it hates you."*

Romans 12:2 (NLT) *"Don't copy the behavior and customs of this world, but let God transform you into a new person by changing the way you think. Then you will learn to know God's will for you, which is good and pleasing and perfect."*

1 John 2:15-16 (NLT) *"Do not love this world nor the things it offers you, for when you love the world, you do not have the love of the Father in you. For the world offers only a craving for physical pleasure, a craving for everything we see, and pride in our achievements and possessions."*

SPIRITUAL FUSION ASSESSMENT

Okay, it is now time to get out your journal and reflect. It is time to be brutally honest with yourself.

1. Do I believe that Satan is very real and that he hates me?
2. Am I Self-Conscience or am I God-Conscience? Am I consumed with my desires, my situation, and my feelings; or am I surrendered to God. Am I seeking out his will and purpose in my life?
3. What areas of my life does Satan have control? Do I allow him to take advantage of my negative emotions? Do I listen to his lies?
4. Am I at a place in my life where I have, or am willing to surrender myself to God's will and purpose for me? Do I trust him enough to do this? If so, am I teachable?

CHAPTER THREE
STUMBLING AND BUMBLING

Many of us seem to stumble and bumble through our lives. One poor choice leads to more poor choices. If we are honest with ourselves, we are usually our own worst enemy. We simply forget to seek out God when making life choices and decisions. Before you know it, one can find themselves quite lost, bitter and feeling out of control.

What is in a person's heart will determine their character. We will battle The Old Man, (the flesh), until we enter eternity. If an individual is teachable and seeks out truth, I believe this is where the will to persevere is birthed. So even in the midst of chaos this person can and will discover truth, meaning and purpose for their life.

For me, my truth is grounded in Christ and his teachings. It is grounded in His promises. My truth, although I am unable to prove his existence, is grounded in my relationship with Christ.

TEST OF FAITH

Test of faith
Test of faith
Oh this life is a test of faith
Walk the line
Don't straddle the fence
Test of faith
Test of faith
Oh this life is a test of faith

When he was eleven
He knelt at the alter
He asked Jesus to come into his life
Asked Jesus to forgive him of his sin

Test of faith
Test of faith
Oh this life is a test of faith
Walk the line
Don't straddle the fence
Test of faith
Test of faith
Oh this life is a test of faith

When he turned sixteen
He started drink'n that liquor
Chase'n the girls
He'd forgotten Jesus
And all about that alter

Test of faith
Test of faith
Oh this life is a test of faith
Walk the line

Don't straddle the fence
Test of faith
Test of faith
Oh this life is a test of faith

By seventeen
He was a daddy
Now he had a bride
And a new little baby girl

He worked real hard
And he finished high school
Took care of his family
And he tried to stay real cool

Test of faith
Test of faith
Oh this life is a test of faith
Walk the line
Don't straddle the fence
Test of faith
Test of faith
Oh this life is a test of faith

Well they packed up what little they had
And started a new life in the big big city

He said Jesus told him to be a preacher man
So he enrolled in college
And got a job

Test of faith
Test of faith
Oh this life is a test of faith
Walk the line

Don't straddle the fence
Test of faith
Test of faith
Oh this life is a test of faith

Well late one night
He got a call
So he rushed back home
As quick as he could
Three days later they buried his mom

Things, they got tough
The fragile marriage,
It came apart
He dropped out of college
And forgot all about that alter

Test of faith
Test of faith
Oh this life is a test of faith
Walk the line
Don't straddle the fence
Test of faith
Test of faith
Oh this life is a test of faith

So he moved back
To his little home town
And stayed with his father
And once again
He knelt at that alter
Well he found a job
Stock'n shelves
And got his own place

He met a new woman
And thought it was love
And soon they were married

He worked real hard
And as time went by...
He realized she was only filling a void
Once again he forgot all about that alter

He ran around and started to drink
Once again, things on the brink

Test of faith
Test of faith
Oh this life is a test of faith
Walk the line
Don't straddle the fence
Test of faith
Test of faith
Oh this life is a test of faith

Jesus was there
All along you see

There came a time
He hit the wall
His heart finally broken
Broken wide open
Down he went
Down to his knees
Then and there he begged God
For his gracious peace
He never did become that preacher – man
He never did get that college degree
And of course
He stumbles daily
Just like you and me.

Test of faith
Test of faith
Oh this life is a test of faith
Walk the line
Don't straddle the fence
Test of faith
Test of faith
Oh this life is a test of faith

So you see
He floundered and bumbled
At the start
But daily, surely
Jesus keeps changing his heart

Ecclesiastes 11:5 (NLT) *"Just as you cannot understand the path of the wind or the mystery of a tiny baby growing in its mother's womb, so you cannot understand the activity of God, who does all things."*

Romans 5:3-5 (NLT) *"We can rejoice, too, when we run into problems and trials, for we know that they help us develop endurance. And endurance develops strength of character, and character strengthens our confident hope of salvation. And this hope will not lead to disappointment. For we know how dearly God loves us, because he has given us the Holy Spirit to fill our hearts with his love."*

1Corinthians 10:13 *"The temptations in your life are no different from what others experience. And God is faithful. He will not allow the temptation to be more than you can stand. When you are tempted, he will show you a way out so that you can endure."*

2Corinthians 4:8-9 (NLT) *"We are pressed on every side by troubles, but we are not crushed. We are perplexed, but not driven to despair. We are hunted down, but never abandoned by God. We get knocked down, but we are not destroyed."*

SPIRITUAL FUSION ASSESSMENT

Okay, it is now time to get out your journal and reflect. It is time to be brutally honest with yourself.

1. Am I seeking God out in my daily decisions, or am I over-confident in my own abilities?
2. When the storms of life rain down on me do I:
   a. Fall into anxiety or depression?
   b. Become paralyzed with fear?
   c. Remember God's promises?

   *Remember, these storms develop endurance, and endurance develops strength of character.

3. How do I react when I am confronted with temptation, or when my faith is tested?

   *Always remember to seek out God. He will show you a way out.

CHAPTER FOUR
OBSCURE BAGGAGE

Everyone's life experience is unique. When we begin a relationship with Christ we often bring along a great deal of cumbersome baggage. We simply do not comprehend how to let go of that baggage. All too often some of our baggage has become so integrated into who we are, that we don't even know it is there.

Growing in Christ is a life-long process. Why is it that some folks seem to transform their lives over night when they decide to follow Christ? While others, like myself, fight and claw and resist change right from the get go? The more cluttered your *house* is, the more work is required for cleanup. I brought a lot of baggage into my relationship with Christ, and to make things more complicated, I seemed to accumulate more baggage as I journeyed along.

For me, my life story is proof enough of everything the Bible teaches us of who Christ is. His grace, his love, his patience... his character simply amazes me; hence the classic hymn, "Amazing Grace".

"Amazing grace, how sweet the sound, that saved a wretch like me. I once was lost but now I am found, was blind but now I see.

Was grace that taught my heart to fear, and grace my fears relieved; how precious did that grace appear the hour I first believed.

Through many dangers, toils, and snares, I have already come; 'tis grace has brought me safe thus far, and grace will lead me home.

When we've been there ten thousand years, bright shining as the sun, we've no less days to sing God's praise than when we'd first begun." John Newton 1779

WEARY WARRIOR

Weary warrior
Tired of this fight
Weary warrior
Only wanting what seems right
Wounded warrior
Feeling disillusioned on this cold dark night
Weary warrior
Loss of focus
All seems blurred
Frightened warrior
Dishonored by those you trust
Wounded warrior
Bleeding though you are
Keep on fighting…
You know that you must
The one you serve
He has remained true
He led the way
He has shown you how to fight
He alone has readied you for this war
Fight with all that you have
Fight hard
Fight into your cold dark night
Then home you will go
Home, where all is made right
At home you will rest…
Rest with him,
Rest with him who has never left

Psalm 143:6-8 (NLT) *"I lift my hands to you in prayer. I thirst for you as parched land thirsts for rain. Come quickly, Lord, and*

answer me, for my depression deepens. Don't turn away from me, or I will die. Let me hear of your unfailing love each morning, for I am trusting in you. Show me where to walk, for I give myself to you."

John 6:29 (NLT) *"...This is the only work God wants from you: Believe in the one he has sent."*

2 Corinthians 12:9-10 (NLT) *"Each time he said, "My grace is all you need. My power works best in weakness." So now I am glad to boast about my weaknesses, so that the power of Christ can work through me. That's why I take pleasure in my weaknesses, and in the insults, hardships, persecutions, and troubles that I suffer for Christ."*

DESTINATION

What is it that draws me from afar?
Is this my destination that lays before?
Or is it merely a resting place for this weary head?
Perhaps it's an illusion,
A trick of the mind.
The air is filled with electricity,
The very air I take in
Is saturated with the dazzling aureate of the setting sun.

Am I in a slumber?
And all that I consume
Be only but a dream?
Or be I wide awake,
And all is very real?

Sigh… whether dream or real,
Matters little.
For what *is* real,
And what *is* not?
What I perceive as real,
Is indeed to me.
It matters little how other men may perceive.
And so, I advance…

Proverbs 29:25 (NLT) *"Fearing people is a dangerous trap, but trusting the Lord means safety."*

Galatians 1:10 (NLT) *"Obviously, I'm not trying to win the approval of people, but of God. If pleasing people were my goal, I would not be Christ's servant."*

1Thessalonians 2:4 (NLT) *"For we speak as messengers approved by God to be entrusted with the Good News. Our purpose is to please God, not people. He alone examines the motives of our hearts."*

EYES

The eyes have waned
I no longer fear
My surroundings have become obscured
I sense their lips moving
But only noise vomits from their lips
I do not discern
Allure is no more
Faith and ambition have scurried away
Desire… none
Now well beyond the torment
Well beyond the fear
Numb I have become,
Numb I am…

1Peter 1:13 (NLT) *"So prepare your minds for action and exercise self-control. Put all your hope in the gracious salvation that will come to you when Jesus Christ is revealed to the world."*

Romans 12:2 (NLT) *"Don't copy the behavior and customs of this world, but let God transform you into a new person by changing the way you think. Then you will learn to know God's will for you, which is good and pleasing and perfect."*

Ecclesiastes 7:1-4 (NLT) *"A good reputation is more valuable than costly perfume. And the day you die is better than the day you are born. Better to spend your time at funerals than at parties. After all, everyone dies so the living should take this to heart. Sorrow is better than laughter, for sadness has a refining influence on us. A wise person thinks a lot about death, while a fool thinks only about having a good time."*

REST

If I undertake this thing...
Where will I awaken?
If I awaken at all
What will they say?
What will they do?

So stale,
Too tired to care
I simply need rest...

Oh to lay this lumbering burden down...
How much longer must this linger?
I am exhausted

Have I failed this eternal test?
Please just let me sleep...
I am done.

Psalm 19:7 (NLT) *"The instructions of the Lord are perfect, reviving the soul. The decrees of the Lord are trustworthy, making wise the simple."*

Psalm 23:1-3 (NLT) *"The Lord is my shepherd; I have all that I need. He lets me rest in green meadows; he leads me beside peaceful streams. He renews my strength. He guides me along right paths, bringing honor to his name."*

Jeremiah 31:25 (NLT) *"For I have given rest to the weary and joy to the sorrowing."*

A SIGN

What's my place in this space
That I just seem to consume
Where have I been?
Where am I going?
What am I doing?

I simply do not know
Jesus come to me
Heal this darkened heart
Repair this fractured mind
I'm look'n for a sign

I feel so lost
At times I'm so afraid
Like a child in the dark
I feel I've lost my way
Like a drifting NOMAD in this world
I've gone so astray
Jesus please come to me
Heal this darkened heart
Repair this fractured mind
I'm look'n for a sign
So much of this world
In my head,
In my heart,
The stench of this world
It just won't leave

Jesus please come to me
All of these eyes
They pierce my soul…
What will I say?
I have not a clue

Jesus come to me
Heal this darkened heart
Repair this fractured mind
I'm look'n for a sign.

John 3:16 (NLT) *"For this is how God loved the world: He gave his one and only Son, so that everyone who believes in him will not perish but have eternal life."*

John 14:16-17 (NLT) *"And I will ask the Father, and he will give you another Advocate, who will never leave you. He is the Holy Spirit who leads into all truth. The world cannot receive him, because it isn't looking for him and doesn't recognize him. But you know him, because he lives with you now and later will be in you."*

2 Timothy 3:16 (NLT) *"All scripture is inspired by God and is useful to teach us what is true and to make us realize what is wrong in our lives. It corrects us when we are wrong and teaches us to do what is right."*

1 Corinthians 6:19-20 (NLT) *"Don't you realize that your body is the temple of the Holy Spirit, who lives in you and was given to you by God? You do not belong to yourself, for God bought you with a high price. So you must honor God with your body."*

FLESH

Jesus loves me
This I know
For the Bible
Tells me so

But oh, this flesh
This flesh it won't let me go

I look at this world that is all around me,
And my, how I am blessed

But if I am so blessed,
Them why oh why am I so depressed

I know that Jesus died for me
He forgave me all my sins

But oh, this flesh
This flesh it won't let me go

I say I love Jesus,
I say I will follow Him

But oh, this flesh
This flesh it won't let me go

He walked this earth
In the flesh
He suffered and he died
This I know

But oh, this flesh
This flesh it won't let me go

He rose on that third day just for me,
He rose from the dead
He ascended to Heaven
All this I know
But oh, this flesh
This flesh, it won't let me go

Jesus loves me this I know
For the Bible tells me so,

But oh, this flesh
This flesh, it just won't let me go…

1 John 2:15-17 (NLT) *"Do not love this world nor the things it offers you, for when you love the world, you do not have the love of the Father in you. For the world offers only a craving for physical pleasure, a craving for everything we see, and pride in our achievements and possessions. These are not from the Father, but are from this world. And this world is fading away, along with everything people crave. But anyone who does what pleases God will live forever."*

Galatians 5:19-21 (NLT) *"When you follow the desires of your sinful nature, the results are very clear: sexual immorality, impurity, lustful pleasures, idolatry, sorcery, hostility, quarreling, jealousy, outbursts of anger, selfish ambition, dissension, division, envy, drunkenness, wild parties, and other sins like these. Let me tell you again, as I have before, that anyone living that sort life will not inherit the Kingdom of God."*

Romans 8:7-8 (NLT) *"For the sinful nature is always hostile to God. It never did obey God's laws, and it never will. That's why those who are still under the control of their sinful nature can never please God."*

Isaiah 40: 29-31 (NLT) *"He gives power to the weak and strength to the powerless. Even youths will become weak and tired, and young men will fall in exhaustion. But those who trust in the Lord will find new strength. They will soar high on wings like eagles. They will run and not grow weary. They will walk and not faint."*

HEY MAN!

Hey man,
What's that road you're travel'n down?
Do you know where it leads?
Tell me,
Do you really know
Just where you're goin?

Lots of people,
They thought they knew the route
Those people,
They tried to show the way,
But that road,
It just seemed to go on and on.

Hey man,
What's that road you're travel'n down?
Do you really know where it leads?
Do you even really know where
You're goin?

I tried getting high
To find my way
I tried sex to ease the pain
I ran from family to escape the past
But that road,
It just went on 'n on

Hey man,
What's that road you're travel'n down?
Do you really know where it leads?
Do you even really know where you're goin?

> Hey man,
> What's that road you're stumbl'n down?
>
> It leads to nowhere man…
> It's a dead end trap… Don't be a fool… turn around while you can…

Psalm 25:4 (NLT) *"Show me the right path, O Lord; point out the road for me to follow."*

Psalm 25:8-10 (NLT) *"The Lord is good and does what is right; he shows the proper path to those who go astray. He leads the humble in doing right, teaching them his way. The Lord leads with unfailing love and faithfulness all who keep his covenant and obey his demands."*

Proverbs 11:14 (NLT) *"Without wise leadership, a nation falls; there is safety in having many advisors."*

John 3:16-17 (NLT) *"For this is how God loved the world; He gave his one and only Son, so that everyone who believes in Him will not perish but have eternal life. God sent his Son into the world not to judge the world, but to save the world through him."*

SPIRITUAL FUSION ASSESSMENT

Okay, it is now time to get out your journal and reflect. It is time to be brutally honest with yourself.

1. Are you willing to accept and embrace God's grace for you? Or are you trapped believing you are not worthy of his grace?
2. Look deep within yourself. Are you seeking to please the people in your life, or are you seeking out a life pleasing to God?
3. Do I remember to have an eternal perspective, or instead do I mimic the behaviors and customs of this world?
4. Are you gripping tightly to your worries? Are you learning to trust in Christ to guide you, and provide for you?
    a. Write down some of the worries in your life that you have a difficult time letting go of.
5. In your moments of desperation, when things seem at their bleakest, the Christ follower always has the person of the Holy Spirit living inside of you. He gives wisdom, strength, and discernment. He will guide your way.
    a. Meditate on, or discuss with your study group how this applies to you.

CHAPTER FIVE
CORPORATE CRAFTINESS

Just the simple fact that we are human, means that we hurt each other. Actually, we hurt each other all of the time. The church family is certainly not exempt from this human short-coming. I've met countless people over the years who when asked if they attend church, say in response something like, "I'm a Christian, but I don't go to church anymore." Typically there is a scowl on their face when they utter those words. Or, a cloud of sadness overcomes their disposition. When pressed further on this topic, the most common response is something like, "Those church people are mean!" or "fake, snobs, a bunch of hypocrites, etc."

It's sad, very sad. I myself stopped attending corporate worship for a time because I felt *wronged* by my church family. Regardless of whether or not I was actually wronged or not, is unimportant now.

As I have grown closer to Christ over the years, I have learned a lot of life-lessons. And I must say, that do to my strong-willed nature, these lessons have been very difficult and quite painful. I have been very humbled by those experiences. With being humbled, comes the ability to allow Christ to do a rebuilding within. My perspectives have drastically changed. I don't think as highly of myself as I once did. Through Christ, it is much more natural to be able to love the unlovable. There is a tenderness within that was not present before.

My pride, arrogance, and my immaturity were the primary cause of my great disdain for the church, and Christians in general. "They were the one with the problem, not me!"

We are such unperfected creatures. God is daily teaching me to see the world through the eyes of Jesus. I'm a forgiven screwed up sinner saved by his amazing grace. He has commanded me to love the unlovable. He demands that I put others before myself. That is why **Galatians 2:20** tells us,

> *"My old self has been crucified with Christ. It is no longer I who live, but Christ lives in me. So I live in this earthly body by trusting in the Son of God, who loved me and gave himself for me."* **(NLT)**

This leads us back to our discussion at the beginning of this book; we must daily seek out *Spiritual Fusion* with our Creator in order to be transformed by him into the new child of God that he desires us to be.

HEY PREACHER MAN

Hey preacher man,
You greeted me with a smile.

Hey preacher man,
You took me by the hand.

Hey preacher man,
You took me along your side.

Hey preacher man,
You had somethin' to sell.

Hey preacher man,
You knew that I was buy'n.

Hey preacher man,
I exposed my soul to you.

Hey preacher man,
You sat and smiled.

Hey preacher man,
I confessed all to you.
Hey preacher man,
You let me in.

Hey preacher man,
I didn't see the knife.

Hey preacher man,
You plunged it deep within.

Hey preacher man,
The blood is coursing from me.

Hey preacher man,
Turn around!

Hey preacher man,
How's your new building comin'?

Hey preacher man,
Your head is buried in the sand.

Hey preacher man,
I never stopped bleedin'.

Hey preacher man,
Are you choking on the sand?
Hey preacher man,
That knife, it's still in your hand.

Hey preacher man,
Who can I trust now?

Hey preacher man,
What's your agenda?
Just what is your plan?
Hey preacher man,
Show me your pies and graphs.

Hey preacher man,
I'm standing here all alone…
I'm left here dry and empty…
Hey preacher man…

1 Peter 5:2 (NLT) *Care for the flock that God has entrusted to you. Watch over it willingly, not grudgingly – not for what you will get out of it, but because you are eager to serve God."*

Hebrews 13:17 (NLT) *"Obey your spiritual leaders, and do what they say. Their work is to watch over your souls, and they are accountable to God. Give them reason to do this with joy and not with sorrow. That would certainly not be for your benefit."*

1 Timothy 5:17 (NLT) *"Elders who do their work well should be respected and paid well, especially those who work hard at both preaching and teaching."*

James 3:1-2 (NLT) *"Dear brothers and sisters, not many of you should become teachers in the church, for we who teach will be judged more strictly. Indeed, we all make many mistakes. For if we could control our tongues, we would be perfect and could also control ourselves in every other way."*

Proverbs 29:23 (NLT) *"Pride ends in humiliation, while humility brings honor."*

James 1:19-20 (NLT) *"Understand this, my dear brothers and sisters: You must all be quick to listen, slow to speak, and slow to get angry. Human anger does not produce the righteousness God desires"*

CRASH

Crash and burn
Feel the sting
Chaos all around
Lost in the maze
My mind now in a daze

A few came running
Quietly helping to mend my wounds

Some gazed at me,
They hung their heads
And faded away

Say this can't happen to you?
You know the Christ,
Yeah… I know him too.

Yeah, go to your precious service,
Raise your hands and pray
Spend your time how you like
Say what you will say

The one who gets the bread,
He never said a thing
Too busy building churches
And counting heads.

You think this can't happen?
You still think that you're immune?
For you know the Christ,
Yeah, I know him too.

You act so naïve
You subsist in a bubble
It's time to awaken,
Or you'll be caught,
Standing in your own rubble.
High in the heavens did I soar,
Suddenly, without warning
I did fall
Like a rocket tumbling from the sky,
I simply did not understand why.

No matter what you do
Be sure to keep in step,
Be sure to beat your drum
Don't color outside the lines
Oh, for you know the Christ…
Yeah, I know him too.

You think you're so invincible
You find yourself so very pure
You have it all together
You'll never crash like me.

My ugliness is all there,
My wounds exposed
For all to see
I'm open and I'm honest
You just stand there and stare
It's just too much for you to bare

My recent crash,
It scared you
It made you look away
You were left feeling empty
With nothing left to say

> You think you're immune
> Because you know the Christ?
> The enemy, he simply laughs at you,
>
> I crashed and burned
> High in the heavens did I soar
> Then without warning I did fall
> Like a rocket tumbling from the sky
> I simply did not understand why.
>
> Crash and burn
> Feel the sting
> Chaos all around
> Lost in the maze,
> My mind now in a daze…

Matthew 18:15-17 (NLT) *"If another believer sins against you, go privately and point out the offense. If the other person listens and confesses it, you have won that person back. But if you are unsuccessful, take one or two others with you and go back again, so that everything you say may be confirmed by two or three witnesses. If the person still refuses to listen, take your case to the church. Then if he or she won't accept the church's decision, treat that person as a pagan or a corrupt tax collector."*

Galatians 6:1 (NLT) *"Dear brothers and sisters, if another believer is overcome by some sin, you who are godly should gently and humbly help that person back onto the right path. And be careful not to fall into the same temptation yourself."*

2 Thessalonians 3:14-15 (NLT) *"Take note of those who refuse to obey what we say in this letter. Stay away from them so they will be ashamed. Don't think of them as enemies, but warn them as you would a brother or a sister."*

Romans 12:3-5 (NLT) *"…I give each of you this warning: Don't think you are better than you really are. Be honest in your evaluation of yourselves, measuring yourselves by the faith God has given us. Just as our bodies have many parts and each part has a special function, so it is with Christ's body. We are many parts of one body, and we all belong to each other."*

Proverbs 11:2 (NLT) *"Pride leads to disgrace, but with humility comes wisdom."*

Matthew 18:21-22 (NLT) *"Then Peter came to him and asked, 'Lord, how often should I forgive someone who sins against me? Seven times?' 'No, not seven times,' Jesus replied, "but seventy times seven!"*

SWARM

Do this
Do that
The orders
They bark at you and me
Be this
Be that
They tell us just what to see

I get lost in the frenzy
I get all caught up
I need to get free

They want you and me to conform
Just pump us out
Like a swarm
Out to roam the world

They tell what is right
They tell what is wrong
Tell you how to look
Tell you just how you should feel
But none of this is even real

I want to break free
I *must* break free
I must be true to me

He made me in His image
He made you and me unique
We are not mannequins
He wants the individual
It is Him that we all need to seek

> So I am simply done agreeing
> I am done conforming
> I will seek Him out
> Even if it leaves me a lonely human being

---

1 Peter 1:14 (NLT) *"So you must live as God's obedient children. Don't slip back into your old ways of living to satisfy your own desires. You didn't know any better then. But now you must be holy in everything you do, just as God who chose you is holy."*

1 John 4:1 (NLT) *"Dear friends, do not believe everyone who claims to speak by the Spirit. You must test them to see if the spirit they have comes from God. For there are many false prophets in the world."*

Exodus 23:2 (NLT) *"You must not follow the crowd in doing wrong. When you are called to testify in a dispute, do not be swayed by the crowd to twist justice."*

James 4:4 (NLT) *"You adulterers! Don't you realize that friendship with the world makes you an enemy of God? I say again: If you want to be a friend of the world, you make yourself an enemy of God."*

Isaiah 29:13 (NLT) *"And so the Lord says, 'These people say they are mine. They honor me with their lips, but their hearts are far from me. And their worship of me is nothing but manmade rules learned by rote."*

POUNDING

Do you hear that noise?
The noise of the world
The world all around you

Hear it pounding?

Pounding...
Pounding...
Pounding...

Like the beating of a drum
It's in your head
That noise,
It will not go away

You pretend not to hear it,
You pretend it isn't real

You go on with your day,
Still, the pounding
It goes on

This pounding,
Like a drum inside your head,
It wakes you from your sleep at night

You can pretend it isn't there,
You can pretend it isn't real,
But still
It does not go away

You make certain that you keep busy

Busy with your job
Busy with your books
Busy with your dead religion

Do you hear it pounding?

Pounding...
Pounding...
Pounding...

Like the beating of a drum

There must be more

Your life a barren desert
Searching wondering
Never finding

Pounding...
Pounding...
Pounding...

Like a drum beating in your head
Do you hear that noise?
The noise of the world
The world that is all around you

Mark 4:19 (NLT) *"...but all too quickly the message is crowded out by the worries of this life, the lure of wealth, and the desire for other things, so no fruit is produced."*

Hebrews 12:2 (NLT) *"...keeping our eyes on Jesus, the champion who initiates and perfects our faith. Because of the joy awaiting* *him, he endured the cross, disregarding its shame. Now he is seated in the place of honor beside God's throne."*

Colossians 3:2-3 (NLT) *"Think about the things of heaven, not the things of earth. For you died to this life, and your real life is hidden with Christ in God."*

Proverbs 4:25-27 (NLT) *"Look straight ahead, and fix your eyes on what lies before you. Mark out a straight path for your feet; stay on the safe path. Don't get sidetracked; keep your feet from following evil."*

HUMAN

You told me to put forward my hand,
They crushed it.
You told me to put forward my foot,
They broke it.
You told me to get up,
They knocked me down.
You told me to take a step,
They tripped me.
You told me to get busy,
They told me to rest.
You told me to share,
They took.
You said you would heal,
They bloodied me.
You told me to serve quietly, with humility,
They said I was lazy.
Now here I am,
Bruised
I opened up
They betrayed me
They are just human…
And so am I

Ephesians 4:31-32 (NLT) *"Get rid of all bitterness, rage, anger, harsh words, slander, as well as all types of evil behavior. Instead, be kind to each other, tenderhearted, forgiving one another, just as God through Christ has forgiven you."*

John 15:12 (NLT) *"This is my commandment: Love each other in the same way I have loved you."*

Matthew 5:44-45 (NLT) *"But I say, love your enemies! Pray for those who persecute you! In that way, you will be acting as true children of your Father in heaven. For he gives his sunlight to both the evil and the good, and he sends rain on the just and the unjust alike."*

Luke 6:31 (NLT) *"Do to others as you would like them to do to you. 'If you love only those who love you, why should you get credit for that? Even sinners love those who love them! And if you do good only to those who do good to you, why should you get credit? Even sinners do that much!"*

Philippians 2:3-4 (NLT) *"Don't be selfish; don't try to impress others. Be humble, thinking of others as better than yourselves. Don't look out only for your own interests, but take an interest in others too."*

SPIRITUAL FUSION ASSESSMENT

Okay, it is now time to get out your journal and reflect. It is time to be brutally honest with yourself.

1. Have you ever been hurt by or feel that you were let down by church leadership, or a fellow parishioner?
   a. If so, on a separate piece of paper write down what took place, how you reacted, and what was the final outcome? (If this has not been resolved, then I recommend seeking out a mature spiritual mentor).
2. If you had a Christian friend that was making self-destructive choices, what, if anything would or could you do?
3. As a Christian, have you ever been caught up in a time of self-destructive behavior, or simply going through a very difficult time? If so, were there any Christian friends who came to you to help you, comfort you, and speak truth to you?
4. Do you strictly follow what your church teaches you; or do you study the Bible regularly as you seek out God's truth?
5. Do you love the unlovable?
6. Is there anyone that you have been unwilling to forgive? (Read Mathew 6:9-13)

CHAPTER SIX
BIRTHING PAINS

When I decided to repent of my sin and follow Christ, I did not "count the cost". I heard what I *knew* to be the truth. I asked God for forgiveness and I asked Jesus to be my King, my guide. Early on in my Christ-walk I did not understand the concept of becoming a *disciple* of Christ. In the book of Luke Christ spells out very clearly what it means to be his disciple:

Luke 14:26-28 (NLT) *"If you want to be my disciple, you must hate everyone else by comparison – your father and mother, wife and children, brothers and sisters – yes, even your own life. Otherwise, you cannot be my disciple. And if you do not carry your own cross and follow me, you cannot be my disciple. But don't begin until you count the cost. For who would begin construction of a building without first calculating the cost to see if there is enough money to finish it?"*

In this passage, Jesus is giving us some very straight-forward instruction as to what a disciple is. If you are a Christ-Follower, or are considering following him, then study this passage intently;

- Have I, or am I willing to elevate Christ above everyone and everything in my life?
- Have I counted the cost? Have I truly sat down and meditated on the pleasurable sin in my life that I must now be willing to surrender, in order to become a disciple of Christ?
- Am I willing to pick up my cross and follow him? Am I ready and prepared to endure heartache for the sake of Christ?

Do not confuse your willingness to serve Christ with somehow being *good enough* to enter heaven or that following Christ will be easy. However, it is a hardship with a purpose. When I chose to follow Christ, the sin-nature did not simply evaporate. Instead, so began the internal conflict within my soul. Never forget one of the fundamental truths of the Christian faith found in Ephesians:

Ephesians 2:8 (NLT) *"God saved you by his grace when you believed. And you can't take credit for this; it is a gift from God."*

However, once we choose to follow Christ, James is very explicit about living a life that is very Christ-like.

James 2:14 (NLT) *"What good is it, dear brothers and sisters, if you say you have faith but don't show it by your actions? Can that kind of faith save anyone?*

As a disciple of Christ, I must always, constantly pursue Spiritual Fusion with my Savior.

THIS MAN

A man walked up to me
He asked, "Do you really want to see?"
"What do you mean?"
He told me that he used to be blind like me
Said he could teach me to see.

He told me about this man
Said he'd walked this earth for me.
The people, they didn't like this man
They didn't like what he had to say,
So they nailed him to a tree
And there is where he died for me.
But that man,
He rose up from the dead
And he ascended up to Heaven!

He said this man you see,
Wants to spend eternity with me.
This guy, this man, this one I sing about, is Jesus Christ.

Thank you Jesus for saving my soul,
Thank you Jesus for taking me in.
Thank you, Jesus for loving me so...

Jesus you are awesome,
Jesus, you are everything.

Thank you Jesus; for opening my eyes.

John 3:17 (NLT) *"God sent his Son into the world not to judge the world, but save the world through him."*

Titus 3:5 (NLT) *"…He saved us, not because of the righteous things we had done, but because of his mercy. He washed away our sins, giving us a new birth and new life through the Holy Spirit."*

Romans 10:9 (NLT) *"If you openly declare that Jesus is Lord and believe in your heart that God raised him from the dead, you will be saved."*

SLIVER

Like a sliver of glass
That pricks at a finger,
Your Spirit
Has pricked at my Soul

Living with an Eternal Perspective

Ephesians 5:15-16 (NLT) *"So be careful how you live. Don't live like fools, but like those who are wise. Make the most of every opportunity in these evil days."*

Psalm 144:3-4 (NLT) *"O Lord, what are human beings that you should notice them, mere mortals that you should think about them? For they are like a breath of air; their days are like a passing shadow."*

James 4:13-16 (NLT) *"Look here, you who say, 'Today or tomorrow we are going to a certain town and will stay there a year. We will do business there and make a profit.' How do you know what your life will be like tomorrow? Your life is like the morning fog – it's here a little while, then it's gone. What you ought to say is, 'If the Lord wants us to, we will live and do this or that.' Otherwise you are boasting about your own pretentious plans, and all such boasting is evil."*

NOTHING

He simply stood there
Looking right through me
A blank look upon his pail face

He said his wife
She had had enough
And he just got his papers…
He was going off to war

That ghostly look upon his face.
What did I say?
What did I do?
Nothing…
No, nothing at all

Did I tell him of my savior's love?
Did I offer to take him by my side and pray?
No… nothing,
Nothing at all

He slumbered away
Out of my life
His head hung low
His entire world
Crumbling to pieces

Did I chase after him?
Did I call out his name?
No… nothing,
Nothing at all

Last night the cops,
They came and took him away

Did I visit him in jail?
Did I write him a letter?
No… nothing,
Nothing at all

Jesus forgive me,
Please change this calloused heart of mine
So much less of me,
So much more of you
Help me Jesus,
Help me to do *something*
Instead of *nothing*
Nothing at all…

1 Corinthians 13:3 (NLT) *"If I gave everything I have to the poor and even sacrificed my body, I could boast about it; but if I didn't love others, I would have gained nothing."*

1 Corinthians 13:4-7 (NLT) *"Love is patient and kind. Love is not jealous or boastful or proud or rude. It does not demand its own way. It is not irritable, and it keeps no record of being wronged. It does not rejoice about injustice but rejoices whenever the truth wins out. Love never gives up, never loses faith, is always hopeful, and endures through every circumstance."*

1 John 4:12 (NLT) *"No one has ever seen God. But if we love each other, God lives in us, and his love is brought to full expression in us."*

Galatians 5:14 (NLT) *"For the whole law can be summed up in this one command: 'Love your neighbor as yourself'."*

YOU

What is it I am doing?
What is it that I want?
I cry out
My soul, it trembles
I am so barren
My soul hungers for you
It is you that I crave
It is you that I require
Only you can restore
Only you can make me whole
Only by you oh Lord
Am I made complete

Psalms 107:9 (NLT) *"For he satisfies the thirsty and fills the hungry with good things."*

John 6:35 (NLT) *"Jesus replied, 'I am the bread of life. Whoever comes to me will never be hungry again. Whoever believes in me will never be thirsty'."*

1 John 5:4-5 (NLT) *"For every child of God defeats this evil world, and we achieve this victory through our faith. And who can win this battle against the world? Only those who believe that Jesus is the Son of God."*

CROW

Gazing into the horizon
The beauty of the golden wheat
The horror of the black crow
Their mocking sinister calls

Haunted, yet intrigued
Mesmerized
Advancing
I must advance
Advance like a weathered soldier
Nearly without emotion,
As though duty bound.

Duty bound to whom,
To what...
That small quiet voice...

Who is this small quiet voice?
Experience?
Ignorance?
The Universe?
A dark Enemy?

It all seems irrelevant.
Moving forward is the *only* option...
There is no other course but forward.

Into the golden wheat I enter.
The buzz of the ominous crow
Choking with entirety...

Matthew 4:19-20 (NLT) *"Jesus called out to them, 'Come, follow me, and I will show you how to fish for people!' And they left their nets at once and followed him."*

Jeremiah 29:11 (NLT) *"For I know the plans I have for you,' says the Lord. 'They are plans for good and not for disaster, to give you a future and a hope."*

Romans 11:29 (NLT) *"For God's gifts and his call can never be withdrawn."*

PATH WALKER

I was just a simple Path Walker,
Meandering down The Path.
Little cares or concerns
Did I possess.

Over time, ever so gradually,
I became bored,
What was *not* on The Path,
Intrigued me...

And so, I ventured off The Path,
Mesmerized by all that was not of The Path.

It was but a short time,
Before I realized I had been deceived.

My way was very cumbersome,
Thick with thorns and bramble.
I began to stumble and bumble,
Exhaustion, it set in.

It was apparent now,
That lost I was indeed!

For when you journey from The Path,
The way becomes impossible.

Frantically, I searched in vain for that Path...
The Path I had once journeyed so merrily.

However, The Path, it eluded me....
For I did not know where to look.

I had almost given up,
I had almost lost all hope.
Finding contentment
With simply meandering, lost,
All alone...
Then suddenly,
I took notice of a bright light
Shining through in the distance!

Was there a clearing up ahead?
Possibly a place of solace,
Where I may find rest?

Fighting through the thorn and bramble,
I pushed towards the light...

Finally, now timidly, I approached the source of the light...

Why, it was The Path!

That same Path that so long ago,
I had journeyed upon.

I stepped onto The Path...
I was now back where I belonged,
I felt refreshed, cleansed.
My joy, my hope,
Now restored!

Now, being a Path Walker again,
I journeyed on The Path.
Allowing The Path to lead me.

Whenever I came upon my
Fellow Path Walkers,
I would warn them of my careless ways,

When I had foolishly
Wondered off The Path.
Those who had already
Wondered off The Path
I helped to guide them back.

Have you left The Path?
Have you lost your way?
Seek out the light,
And surely you will find yourself
On The Path once again.

Yes, once again, you will be a Path Walker.

Proverbs 4:26-27 (NLT) *"Mark out a straight path for your feet; stay on the safe path. Don't get sidetracked; keep your feet from following evil."*

Proverbs 16:17 (NLT) *"The path of the virtuous leads away from evil; whoever follows that path is safe."*

Proverbs 3:6 (NLT) *"Seek his will in all you do, and he will show you which path to take."*

Hebrews 12:13 (NLT) *"Mark out a straight path for your feet so that those who are weak and lame will not fall but become strong."*

ALIVE

I stumbled from my slumber
To awaken to a sting
Wide eyed with pain
But now fully awake…

Proverbs 9:10 (NLT) *"Fear of the Lord is the foundation of wisdom. Knowledge of the Holy One results in good judgement."*

Psalm 119:130 (NLT) *"The teaching of your word gives light, so even the simple can understand."*

Psalm 119:105 (NLT) *"Your word is a lamp to guide my feet and a light for my path."*

James 1:18 (NLT) *"He chose to give birth to us by giving us his true word. And we, out of all creation, became his prized possession."*

SPIRITUAL FUSION ASSESSMENT

Okay, it is now time to get out your journal and reflect. It is time to be brutally honest with yourself.

1. Do you ever stop to think just how holy God is? Are you amazed by his infinite vastness? Meditate on God's immense vastness while he simultaneously loves and cares for you intimately.
2. Jesus taught us that the most important attribute we can poses is love. Do you struggle with loving others, especially the unlovable?
3. Have you asked God to show you what his purpose for your life is? (Listen…)
4. Do you avoid toxic people, places, and situations that you know may pull you away from God?
5. We must never forget that our lives are to be an example to others. Like it or not, others are always watching. When you engage in things that you know are unpleasing to God, you may very well be pulling other believers away as well.
6. When "no one is watching", are you still living out what you believe to be truth? Are you doing what you believe to be right before God?

CHAPTER SEVEN
GROWING PAINS

A healthy Christ-centered life is very fulfilling. It brings authentic joy within. When trusting in Christ, he instills confidence. However, if I am going to be totally honest, I also find that being a Christ-follower brings with it a sober-minded sadness to my spirit.

His Spirit has made me so much more aware of the dark and broken world that is all around us. There is this awareness now, that this world is not my home. I am a stranger traveling through. I am reminded by Him that I am to be *in*, not *of* this world.

1 John 2:15-17 (NLT) *"Do not love this world nor the things it offers you, for when you love the world, you do not have the love of the Father in you. For the world offers only a craving for physical pleasure, a craving for everything we see, and pride in our achievements and possessions. These are not from the Father, but are from this world. And this world is fading away, along with everything people crave. But anyone who does what pleases God will live forever."*

The longer I journey with Christ, I am made more aware of my sinful nature, The Old Man. This world is at times simply exhausting, and I find myself longing for my eternal home. Do not misunderstand me, I am not talking about longing for home because I am depressed or overwhelmed – quite the opposite! I believe in my God's eternal promises so much; how could I *not* look forward to my eternal home!

However, while I am here, there is much work to be done in His service. The entire reason you and I were created was to bring our Creator pleasure. So, I am constantly, though I fall short regularly, seeking out Spiritual Fusion with Christ.

TORMENTED

When things eternal
Stretch me wide
When my mind is filled to its limits
When my soul quakes with eternal wonderings...
I am tormented.

Then tormented may I be!
For I would rather be tormented
As I wrestle these eternal thoughts and concepts
As I struggle with the conflict within,
As I squeeze these eternal wonderings,
As I contemplate my fate.

Oh, to experience this insignificant struggle
Than to find myself in slumber
And suffer eternal turmoil...
How very ironic indeed!

John 8:32 (NLT) *"And you will know the truth, and the truth will set you free."*

John 4:24 (NLT) *"For God is Spirit, so those who worship him must worship in spirit and truth."*

Hebrews 4:12 (NLT) *"For the word of God is alive and powerful. It is sharper than the sharpest two-edged sword, cutting between soul and spirit, between joint and marrow. It exposes our innermost thoughts and desires."*

ESSENCE

Cruis'n along just liv'n
Liv'n out this life you've given

I was pondering the vastness of your greatness
Then suddenly,

You stopped me cold –
You stopped me dead in my tracks
The world all around
Coming to a halt…

Your voice oh so very tender…
Like a romantic melody
A voice like thunder…
Commanding and reverent

"See me"
"Know me"
The sky black with night
In a flash
Revealing yourself to me

"Look that you may see"

His abdomen, a mighty hurricane
No ship could ever sail

A storm that shook the very foundations of Hell
Blacker than the night
More fierce and relentless than the cold vastness of space

Nothing able to escape his might
Not even the creatures swimming
The deepest depths
Could escape his sight

His chest was a vast blue sea of infinity
A sea so colossal
It could never be contained
Not even the universe
Could imprison this infinite sea!

All of these wonders
My minds' eye witnessed
In an instant of time

If more had been revealed
My soul would have leapt
From this mortal shell of mine

Then I heard him say,
"This is less than a droplet of Myself"

The tears burst from my eyes
Speech, it would not come…
Awe, reverence, and silence for my Lord on High

I had been invited
To the Holy of Holies
I was literally in His presence
I had been given just a glimpse of His very essence

I wept uncontrollably
His glory,
His might,
They overwhelmed me

It seemed He stepped back
Oh so very gently
I felt His kind smile

Softly, tenderly, He said,
"I know my child, I know"

Like a shepherd
Aiding a frightened bleating lamb
His love loomed over me
Shading me from the night

How wonderful,
How very terrible
Oh how gentle
Oh how so very fierce

I heard this thing coming
Like a million-man army
Thunderous marching
Coming this way
I felt the vibrations
I sensed its coming

God forbid that I ever forget
That oh so wonderful
Yet horrific morn
That we met

I will forever be changed
From this event
That I am most certain
Was heaven sent

1 Samuel 2:2 (NLT) *"No one is holy like the Lord! There is no one besides you; there is no Rock like our God."*

Isaiah 57:15 (NLT) *"The high and lofty one who lives in eternity, the Holy One, says this: 'I live in the high and holy place with those whose spirits are contrite and humble. I restore the crushed spirit of the humble and revive the courage of those with repentant hearts'."*

Psalm 96:9 (NLT) *"Worship the Lord in all his holy splendor. Let all the earth tremble before him."*

TRANSMUTED

As I fell upon my sword
I cried out to my Lord
So self-righteous I had become
My poor choices
Like corpses
Strung about
Smell of death in the air

Fractured hearts
Fractured minds
Fractured lives

Each life is a theatre of battle
Each life riddled with chaotic free will

Grotesque words spew forth
Like shots ringing out

Piercing hearts
Piercing minds
Piercing lives

Perspectives forevermore transmuted
The armor thickens
Thickens as the bullets fly

Masked in obscurity
The shrapnel scorches
It burns
It scares

All is raw
Exposed
Naked we become

Vulnerability is what heals
Calm…
A stillness in the air
Stripped of all
Brokenness…

Taking notice
Not looking past
No longer seeing thru
Now peering within

This new insight within,
It carries pain
It brings sorrow
Peering within brings me to my knees

What once was hawkish and calloused
Now has become tender and docile
As I gradually expire,
I now come to life

Eternally transmuted

2 Corinthians 3:18 (NLT) *"So all of us who have had that veil removed can see and reflect the glory of the Lord. And the Lord – who is the Spirit – makes us more and more like him as we are changed into his glorious image."*

2 Corinthians 5:17 (NLT) *"This means that anyone who belongs to Christ has become a new person. The old life is gone; a new life has begun!"*

Galatians 2:20 (NLT) *"My old self has been crucified with Christ. It is no longer I who live, but Christ lives in me. So I live in this earthly body by trusting in the Son of God, who loved me and gave himself for me."*

1 Corinthians 15:51 (NLT) *"But let me reveal to you a wonderful secret. We will not all die, but we will all be transformed."*

REALITY

Life is an irony
Time is a lie
Many truths are untrue

What is reality?
What is not?
Is it what I can touch?
Is it what I can see?
It would seem not to me

2 Peter 3:8 (NLT) "But you must not forget this one thing, dear friends: A day is like a thousand years to the Lord, and a thousand years is like a day."

James 4:14 (NLT) *"How do you know what your life will be like tomorrow? Your life is like the morning fog – it's here a little while, then it's gone."*

Hebrews 11:1 (NLT) *"Faith is the confidence that what we hope for will actually happen; it gives us assurance about things we cannot see."*

Ecclesiastes 3:11 (NLT) *"Yet God has made everything beautiful for its own time. He has planted eternity in the human heart, but even so, people cannot see the whole scope of God's work from beginning to end."*

Colossians 3:1-3 (NLT) *"Since you have been raised to new life with Christ, set our sights on the realities of heaven, where Christ sits in the place of honor at God's right hand."*

SOLACE

I just sit
And I think
I contemplate poor choices
My past comes at me
And I sit, and I think
In solace I think
I think of harsh words spoken
Of things not said
I want to reach out.
To tell you it's okay
In solace I think
I dream of no loneliness
I think of no pain
I think of sunshine
I feel the warm summer breeze
I just sit
And I think
In solace, I think

---

1 Corinthians 13:12 (NLT) *"Now we see things imperfectly, like puzzling reflections in a mirror, but then we will see everything with perfect clarity. All that I know now is partial and incomplete, but then I will know everything completely."*

Psalms 19:14 (NLT) *"May the words of my mouth and meditation of my heart be pleasing to you, O Lord, my rock and my redeemer."*

Revelation 21:4 (NLT) *"He will wipe every tear from their eyes, and there will be no more death or sorrow or crying or pain. All these things are gone forever."*

BIG BIG GLASS

What have I obtained?
What have I been given?
Just what is it that I've received?
Staring off over there,
Glances all around…
What is it I've thrown away?
Need me some good lovin',
Just leave me alone.
Drinking from a big big glass,
Now that's real nice.
Do you hear that?
Of course you don't.
Oh man, the sun went down,
Went down a long time ago.
Don't cry about it,
Just stumble in the dark…
That's what we do,
Drink from a big big glass,
Then we stumble in the dark.
I didn't mean to step on you,
Honest I didn't.
Will the sun rise again?
Drinking from a big big glass,
Just waiting for the dawn…
Gripping my big big glass.

Ecclesiastes 1:2-4 (NLT) *"Everything is meaningless," says the Teacher, "completely meaningless!" What do people get for all their hard work under the sun? Generations come and generations go, but the earth never changes. The sun rises and the sun sets, then hurries around to rise again."*

Luke 12:15 (NLT) *"Then he said, 'Beware! Guard against every kind of greed. Life is not measured by how much you own'."*

1 Peter 2:11 (NLT) *"Dear friends, I warn you as "temporary residents and foreigners" to keep away from worldly desires that wage war against your very souls."*

THE DANCE

Faceless, they are coalesced
Life and death
There is no detaching
They house these mortal shells

They are joined,
As in a Dance
This Dance we call life

At first faceless,
Virtually formless

One may see beauty,
Another is repulsed
One experiencing bliss,
Another, only misery
Another detached, disengaged
Each has their own perspective
This great Dance that we call life,
It plays out before us

Each viewing so diversely
Choose to take part in this eternal Dance
This Dance that you were birthed into
Engage…
Savor it

Recognize the allure,
The artistry,
The tender elegance

At times, dancing as a solitary figure,
At times, entwined in the dance of others

Engage...
Savor...
The Dance

Proverbs 4:6-9 (NLT) *"Don't turn your back on wisdom, for she will protect you. Love her, and she will guard you. Getting wisdom is the wisest thing you can do! And whatever else you do, develop good judgment. If you prize wisdom, she will make you great. Embrace her, and she will honor you. She will place a lovely wreath on your head; she will present you with a beautiful crown."*

Colossians 3:23-24 (NLT) *"Work willingly at whatever you do, as though you were working for the Lord rather than for people. Remember that the Lord will give you an inheritance as your reward, and that the Master you are serving is Christ."*

Philippians 4:8 (NLT) *"And now, dear brothers and sisters, one final thing. Fix your thoughts on what is true, and honorable, and right, and pure, and lovely, and admirable. Think about things that are excellent and worthy of praise."*

HAUNTED

Death dances around in my mind
Mother so vigorous with love and life
A passionate magnet to all in her presence.
Why was I so compelled?
Why did I think it would help?
As I gently kissed her cheek
While her lifeless body lay in that box
It was not her that I kissed
But merely a cold lifeless shell
A shell to what was once so beautiful
Now that shell haunts me
Haunts me as she dances forever in my mind

What of the precious lifeless babe
The babe that I pulled from a mother's arms
A mother, who's mind was now fractured
Unable to discern…
The feel of this cold stiff lifeless infant in my arms
The chilling screams of a brokenhearted mother
Mother and baby will forever haunt me
Together they haunt me.
Haunt as they dance forever in my mind.

There is great purpose to this walk
Life is not simply a random order of events.
The farther I walk,
I am sobered
The flippant emotions of youth
They fade with each step

> A melancholy peace simmers in my soul
> A letting go is shaping, forming
> I am broken
> And broken is good…

Psalms 34:18-20 (NLT) *"The Lord is close to the brokenhearted; he rescues those whose spirits are crushed. The righteous person faces many troubles, but the Lord comes to the rescue each time. For the Lord protects the bones of the righteous; not one of them is broken!"*

John 12:24 (NLT) *"I tell you the truth, unless a kernel of wheat is planted in the soil and dies, it remains alone. But its death will produce many new kernels – a plentiful harvest of new lives."*

James 4:6 (NLT) *"And he gives grace generously. As the Scriptures say, 'God opposes the proud but gives grace to the humble'."*

1 Peter 5:7 (NLT) *"Give all your worries and cares to God, for he cares about you."*

Isaiah 53:5-6 (NLT) *"But he was pierced for our rebellion, crushed for our sins. He was beaten so we could be whole. He was whipped so we could be healed. All of us, like sheep, have strayed away. We have left God's paths to follow our own. Yet the Lord laid on him the sins of us all."*

SPIRITUAL FUSION ASSESSMENT

Okay, it is now time to get out your journal and reflect. It is time to be brutally honest with yourself.

1. If you are a Christ Follower, are you learning how to live *in* the world, without being *of* the world?
2. Have you discovered new found freedoms as you experience God's truths? Explain what that means to you, and how it has changed your perspective on life.
3. In your quiet time with God, are you seeking to go deep? Are you being completely honest with yourself and with God?
4. Do you enjoy the fruits of your hard work without falling in love with this world?
5. Do you actively seek out and ask God for his wisdom?
6. When you perform tasks, are you aiming to please God, or are you simply attempting to please people?
7. Would you say that you are a humble person? Do you think that your classmates, coworkers, or family members would say that you are a humble person?
8. Reflect back on a traumatic event from your past. Have you taken the wounds from that event to God? Have you asked him to help heal you?

CHAPTER EIGHT
AGED HUMILITY

I enjoy a good red wine. Preferably a nice Merlot, or Cabernet. And while I enjoy the warm rush as the wine enters my gullet, this by no means makes me a wine connoisseur. I read somewhere once that not all wines improve with age, however, other wines improve immensely as they are aged.

This seems to be true with people as well! I have a quiet way of approaching people; the older you are, the higher my expectations are of you. That is why it is such a wonderful experience to meet a young adult who is wise and mature "beyond their years". When I meet a young adult who is humble, and teachable it simply lifts my spirit. However, when I meet someone who is getting along in years, and they are loud, brash, opinionated, etc.… I want to run! Likewise, when I'm around an older person and they seem beaten down, and worn out from life, maybe even bitter, well… I also have the urge to bolt. I don't want to be marinated in their negativity.

The point of all of this is this: Life is a training ground. We are eternal creatures. We are simply being readied for the rest of eternity. Our minds simply cannot comprehend this. Think of your physical life here on earth as boot-camp. Every single life experience is preparing you for eternity. What we do with this life, how we "handle" this life, shapes us and molds our eternity.

Hebrews 13:14 (NLT) *"For this world is not our permanent home, we are looking forward to a home yet to come."*

Like wine, some people age well. These people are humbled by life. These people never stop being students. These are the individuals who move through life, some quietly, some ferociously, with an admirable strength. Sadly, many people, like some wine, do not age well at all. These people seem to make the same mistakes over and over again. These people are not teachable, or humble. These people have become "victims" of circumstance. These sad souls are beaten and bitter.

Each person has a choice, a free-will. I have made so many terrible mistakes throughout my life. Many of these mistakes have caused much pain and sorrow. But until I was humbled and became teachable, my life was a wreck.

When I simply said, "God, I can't do this anymore. Please help me, change me, forgive me, teach me…" this is when, very slowly, a wonderful transformation began to take place.

This is what I am referring to when I speak of seeking out Spiritual Fusion between myself and the Creator. This does not happen overnight. This growth and transformation is a lifelong process as we prepare for eternal life.

So, take each day with baby steps. Own your mistakes. Allow life to humble you. Be teachable. Above all, seek out Spiritual Fusion with your Creator.

SEEKING...

I seek peace... yet I am quick to anger
I seek love... yet I will hold a grudge
I seek direction... and yet I am lost
I desire wisdom... and I am but a fool
I chase knowledge... and yet I am rash
I am a dreamer... yet I am a realist
I am a nomad... but I find myself grounded
I perceive my life eternally... yet I am confined by time
I love the artist... yet I am despised by the brush
I embrace the musician... yet I cannot play
I seek tranquility... yet the beating drum continues
I seek out humility... yet, I draw attention
I am bold ... and therefor I am scorned
I seek meaning... and this world offers little
I study... and I am left with more questions
The religious... they find me awkward
The worldly... they find me awkward as well
I am independent... I have a servant's heart
I am a leader... usually I am led to follow
I desire to be quiet... yet my voice cries out
I seek rest, for I am so weary
I seek contentment... I find that I am restless
I scorn those who judge me... yet I condemn
I am blessed to serve... I find it awkward to be served
I am cautious of others... I want to be trusted
I am a free spirit... I seek structure
My soul cries out... at times it screams out
I will not stop questioning...
I will not,
I cannot...
To do so, would be my demise

2 Corinthians 4:16 (NLT) *"That is why we never give up. Though our bodies are dying, our spirits are being renewed every day".*

1 Corinthians 15:51 (NLT) *"But let me reveal to you a wonderful secret. We will not all die, but we will all be transformed!"*

Proverbs 18:15 (NLT) *"Intelligent people are always ready to learn. Their ears are open for knowledge".*

James 1:17 (NLT) *"Whatever is good and perfect is a gift coming down to us from God our Father, who created all the lights in the heavens. He never changes or casts a shifting shadow".*

Hebrews 5:11-14 (NLT) *"… especially since you are spiritually dull and don't seem to listen. You have been believers so long now that you ought to be teaching others. Instead, you need someone to teach you again the basic things about God's word. You are like babies who need milk and cannot eat solid food. For someone who lives on milk is still an infant and doesn't know how to do what is right. Solid food is for those who are mature, who through training have the skill to recognize the difference between right and wrong."*

EGO

What was once new and bright
Those ambitions that I prized so very much…
Held deeply within my heart
That which I craved the very most
Those things which I found insatiable;

Those things are now relics
Just stuff
Stuff of little or no concern
They matter little or not at all
Those things have tarnished,
Faded or have been extinguished

What I grasped oh so tightly,
What I valued so highly
These things are no longer
And matter little, if at all

Those items,
Whether be conceptual or tangible,
All youthful stupidity
Idealistic, unlearned, lacking depth and experience.

As I age
It is made clear to me
How very little I actually know.
And in this there is freedom
In this, there is growth.
Through this I truly become the student
By this, wisdom is freely delivered

> In all of this,
> I find peace
> Through this, ego is put to death.

Proverbs 23:15-16 (NLT) *"My child, if your heart is wise, my own heart will rejoice! Everything in me will celebrate when you speak what is right".*

Matthew 6:21 (NLT) *"Wherever your treasure is, there the desires of your heart will also be".*

Luke 6:40 (NLT) *"Students are not greater than their teacher. But the student who is fully trained will become like the teacher".*

Philippians 2:3-7 (NLT) *"Don't be selfish; don't try to impress others. Be humble, thinking of others as better than yourselves. Don't look out only for your own interests, but take an interest in others, too. You must have the same attitude that Christ Jesus had. Though he was God, he did not think of equality with God as something to cling to. Instead, he gave up his divine privileges; he took the humble position of a slave and was born as a human being…"*

GIANTS

My reflective spirit is like that of thunderous giants
Methodically approaching from a great distance.
Their monstrous gate indicating great change in the air.
These giants draped in change,
Indifferent to good or ill.
Their only concern,
Their purpose,
Is to bring change.
They are blind to whom this change may consume.
It simply falls upon the consumed,
Whether this change be deemed ill-fated or for prosperity.
Each individual must embrace these giants
Without blame,
Without victimization.
To strive to be noble,
To rise above,
To gladly embrace those giants.
Seek to move through this life wide awake.
Do not slumber
Do not sleepwalk
Through this one eternal life you have been given.
We are eternal creatures.
The greatest sin of all is a dull, slothful, self-indulgent life.

James 5:11 (NLT) *"We give great honor to those who endure under suffering. For instance, you know about Job, a man of great endurance. You can see how the Lord was kind to him at the end, for the Lord is full of tenderness and mercy".*

Proverbs 23:20-21 (NLT) *"Do not carouse with drunkards or feast with gluttons, for they are on their way to poverty, and too much sleep clothes them in rags".*

1Peter 4:1-2 (NLT) *"So then, since Christ suffered physical pain, you must arm yourselves with the same attitude he had, and be ready to suffer too. For if you have suffered physically for Christ, you have finished with sin".*

Mathew 23:25 (NLT) *"What sorrow awaits you teachers of religious law and you Pharisees. Hypocrites! For you are so careful to clean the outside of the cup and the dish, but inside you are filthy-full of greed and self-indulgence!"*

SUBLIME FACELESS

Sublime faceless weighing down on me
My gait is wayward and they know

Is wayward my way?
It would seem

I woke up inside my dream
The faceless were checking in

They swarmed about me
Speaking with no voice
Questioning my wayward ways

I scrutinized their gaze
I knew their faceless haughty thought

My gait is queer
I do not harmonize
I find their melody distasteful
They find me wayward,
Awkward, inept…

I do not like the Sublime Faceless
They do not care for me

They are colorless,
Lacking melody
Their thought is drab

I slipped away
With my wayward gait
The harmony inside… I like.

> This place, those Faceless Sublime, all vapor;
>
> I am only here for a time…

Proverbs 21:24 (NLT) *"Mockers are proud and haughty; they act with boundless arrogance."*

Proverbs 16:5 (NLT) *"The Lord detests the proud; they will surely be punished."*

1 Corinthians 2:1 (NLT) *"When I first came to you, dear brothers and sisters, I didn't use lofty words and impressive wisdom to tell you God's secret plan."*

Psalms 18:27 (NLT) *"You rescue the humble, but you humiliate the proud."*

SPIRITUAL FUSION ASSESSMENT

Okay, it is now time to get out your journal and reflect. It is time to be brutally honest with yourself.

1. Once again, look deep within yourself and be honest.
   a. Are you teachable?
   b. Are you growing?
   c. Are you a student of life; seeking out ultimate truth.
2. There are so many blessings in our day-to-day lives that are easily taken for granted. Take time out to thank God for your blessings.
3. What is it that you treasure most? Remember, God tells us we are to put no one and nothing before him.
4. Suffering comes to everyone at some point in life. During times of suffering do you turn to God?
5. Regardless of your age, are you selective about who you spend your free time with? Avoid toxic people and toxic situations. Do not allow yourself to be marinated in their negativity.
6. Are you comfortable being yourself around anyone and everyone?

CHAPTER NINE
JOURNEY'S END

The Bible actually makes it quite clear why we were created... why *you* were created. What is the purpose of life? Why am I here? Why was I created? First of all, it begins with me understanding and accepting the fact that I was not created for *me*. I was not created to spend my entire life seeking out my carnal pleasures and desires.

Colossians 1:16-17 (NLT) *"...Everything was created through him and for him. He existed before anything else, and he holds all creation together."*

Proverbs 16:4 (NLT) *"The Lord has made everything for his own purposes..."*

God made me to bring him pleasure. He is pleased when I surrender my life to him by accepting his grace, and his unconditional love. When I say, "Yes Lord please take me as I am, a sinner, my life is yours..." When I realize that my life is not my own, then a very real life with eternal perspective begins.

This is when seeking out Spiritual Fusion with the Creator of the universe begins.

Who am I to question God?

Psalms 103:14 (NLT) *"For he knows how weak we are; he remembers we are only dust."*

After all, the Creator of the universe says that he knows and cares for me intimately. Read Psalms 139 in its entirety. In fact read Psalms 139 daily as part of your prayer time with God. Consider this; the Creator of everything, the Beginning and the End, the One who was not created, the One who has always been, knows every intimate detail about you, and desires a relationship with you.

This belief, this surrendering of ourselves to Christ requires faith.

Hebrews 11:1 (NLT) *"Faith is the confidence that what we hope for will actually happen; it gives us assurance about things we cannot see."*

Simply put; I am not an apologist, I do not debate or defend my faith. I know what I believe and it is my life's ambition to seek him and his truth's out until my journey on this earth is completed.

THE CAPTAIN

Well, I received a letter in the mail the other day,
It said that I was invited to come and sail away.
It said this wouldn't be "your typical cruise",
This would be an old sailing ship
And there would be work that I would have to do.
This trip would be difficult
If I accepted this invitation,
I would be challenged and pushed like never before.
The letter said that I should think it through
That I should count the cost

Well, I stood there, letter in hand…
Contemplating
Reflecting on my life
Deliberating
Weighing the good and the bad…
My mood quite pensive.

Suddenly, "I will go!"

Now in the letter it was ever so clear;
I must sell everything,
I would not be coming back.
Though the journey promised to be difficult,
The reward it promised,
Far exceeded the hardships that it would entail.

The following morn
I arrived at the pier.
There she was…
My heart racing,
I approached the old sailing ship.
She was quite modest, though a beauty to behold

As I stepped onto the gangway
Carrying all the luggage I could manage,
I was greeted by the Captain.

He raised his hand at me.
Softly, yet with authority
He said, "Leave that baggage behind,
On this journey it will only interfere."

A bit dismayed,
I simply did not know what to say.
He simply smiled and said,
"If you're going on this voyage you must put your trust in me."
Pausing, feeling a bit fearful,
His gaze still fixed upon me,
I unexplainably trusted him.
I dropped my baggage,
And aboard I came.

As I boarded the mystic vessel
Its immense size was realized.
I observed all of my new shipmates
Already on board and hard at work.

They were much like me;
Some of them were thin,
And some were fat.
Some had long hair,
Some had none at all.
They were of all ages,
Short and tall.

There was a commonality that ran through this crew,
We all had left that old world behind.
Most had left their baggage at the dock,
But a few simply couldn't let go.

At this point the Captain,
He gathered us all around.
He said, "This voyage that we are about to begin,
It will not be easy,
But I'll be with you at the end."
He told us not to worry,
Said no matter what,
He would be there for us,
All that we'd have to do is ask.

He said that some of us wouldn't finish,
There would be those who thought they know better.
However, those who complete this difficult voyage,
Our reward would be waiting...

So I pledged to the Captain,
Right there and then,
"I will complete this journey,
I'm with you 'till the end!"

At last we set sail.
Oft to sea we went.
The morning sun shining in all its glory,
The water a brilliant blue,
The salt air...
I simply sighed
Taking in that view.

Things went rather smoothly,
For what seemed quite a while.
Everyone assigned a task
Everyone with his job to do.

As the journey took us farther out to sea,
The water, it began to get rough.

The winds picked up,
The vessel, it began to toss and turn,
The sky became angry and very dark.

Like ravenous timber wolves,
The wind came howling in the night.
And oh how the lightning it did crash.
That now seemingly tiny vessel danced all about.

Well I, and my shipmates,
We had about as much as we could take.
One by one, each of us
Well, we cowered below deck.

The Captain
He had told us that when we hit a storm,
Each of us would have a job to do
And to leave the rest to him.

But no, not one of us had much concern for his assignment
On that stormy night!
Instead we cowered together
Hiding below deck
Just contemplating our doom.

As we all stood there,
Huddled in fear,
The Captain, he walked in.
He surveyed the dark damp hold…
The Captain,
He was as calm as calm could be.
His disposition was one of control and action
He had a smile on his face,
And well, he was softly humming as he walked.

He approached each of us
One by one…
He placed his weathered hand upon my shoulder.
His grasp was firm,
Somehow encouraging.
He calmly said,
"I told you that I'd never leave you
You can put your faith in me
Why, I'd even give my life
In order to save yours you see."

He peered into my eyes
He asked me,
"Do you trust me?"
"Yes I do!" I said.
"Then go back up on that deck,
For you have a task to do."

So one by one, every man in that hold,
We ventured back up to the deck.
And though that fierce storm crashed all about,
Each man focused on his task at hand.
That storm ended…
As storms always do.

So, on that voyage we continued.
We lost track of time as each man carried out his task
Day by day passed
With the occasional storm raging at us.
And though it wasn't easy,
This new way of life,
Well, I knew it was better.

The Captain, he proved to be right;
There were some deserters,

JOURNEY'S END

There were those who could no longer stand this voyage,
They no longer wanted any part of it.

There were even some,
That plotted against our dear Captain
They said he was mad,
They said he was trouble.
They schemed and they planned,
They wanted him dead.

Late one night,
Near journeys end,
They plotted together.
They rushed my dear Captain.
They bound him with rope.
Without even a struggle,
Without one ill word from his lips
They threw my dear captain into the sea.

I watched in horror,
But I hid and did nothing
I coward in a corner
And wept bitterly 'till morning.

Those of us who loved and served the Captain,
We swore we'd honor him with our lives.
So for the remainder of that voyage
We each lived and worked as he had instructed.

At last the arduous journey came to an end
As we ran ashore on a beautiful isle.

As we unloaded that vessel,
At the end of the plank,
There stood my Captain
With a festive countenance all about.

He took my hand with tears of joy,
"Well done, good and faithful servant."
I collapsed to my knees, and we embraced.
As we let go of one another
And I walked on into that paradise,
The Captain had a sad look appear upon his face…

As he turned his attention to another,
I heard him mournfully say,
"I never knew you."

Matthew 7:21-23 (NLT) *"Not everyone who calls out to me, 'Lord! Lord!' will enter the Kingdom of Heaven. Only those who actually do the will of my Father in heaven will enter. On judgment day many will say to me, 'Lord! Lord! We prophesied in your name and cast out demons in your name.' But I will reply, 'I never knew you. Get away from me, you who break God's laws'."*

2 Corinthians 12:4 (NLT) *"…I was caught up to paradise and heard things so astounding that they cannot be expressed in words, things no human is allowed to tell."*

Colossians 3:2-3 (NLT) *"Think about the things of heaven, not the things of earth. For you died to this life, and your real life is hidden with Christ in God."*

Hebrews 12:14 (NLT) *"Work at living in peace with everyone, and work at living a holy life, for those who are not holy will not see the Lord."*

Romans 14:17 (NLT) *"For the Kingdom of God is not a matter of what we eat or drink, but of living a life of goodness and peace and joy in the Holy Spirit."*

SPIRITUAL FUSION ASSESSMENT

Okay, it is now time to get out your journal and reflect. It is time to be brutally honest with yourself.

1. Without behaving "religiously" and without being obnoxious and arrogant, are you seeking out a holy lifestyle i.e. Spiritual Fusion?
2. Are you at peace with those in your life? Is there anyone that you have not forgiven?

CHAPTER TEN
SALT AIR

Jesus is my Lord and Savior. Without him I was so lost and confused. He has brought not only meaning into my life, but stability and strength as well. As I seek out Spiritual Fusion, he slowly, patiently transforms my mind. The daily life struggles still exist, but they no longer weigh me down as they once did. Christ offers a new perspective of what is important. He is teaching me not to worry and fret over the things which I have no control over. And likewise I am learning to take all of my decisions to him. Christ is becoming the navigator of my life.

With Christ leading my life, there is a silent strength and joy that he provides even during life's most difficult times. As he transforms my mind, I am learning to lean on my faith in him and his Word, rather than leaning on my emotions. I find that I'm not so quick to let my emotions control my decision making. This change, has rid my life of the crazy chaos that it once was. I ask for Godly wisdom, he grants it.

Do you know who you are? Do you like who you are? Do you love yourself?

Take a good long look at yourself. Do you understand your personality type? Do you know your likes and dislikes? What are you good at?

In my studies, I read a book entitled, "Wired That Way" by author, Marita Littauer. In her book, she writes;

> *"Have you ever noticed that there are people out there who are different from you? Perhaps you live with them. Maybe you work with them.... We all come with our own personality, determined before birth within our individual genetic makeup. Environment plays a role in how that personality is shaped, but the basics are predetermined".*

There have been many books written about *personality types*. However, I have never read one of these books that has helped me to understand myself and those around me with the depth that Ms. Littauer was able to describe in her book. Reading her book will equip the reader with the ability to understand why we all need to be wired differently. Her book will help you to embrace others unique actions and reactions to daily living. As we learn this new perspective, it is then that we begin to see and love others through the eyes of Christ.

God created you for a purpose. There is none other like you in all of creation. Meditate on that thought for a moment. You were not randomly made,

Psalms 139:14 (NLT) *"Thank you for making me so wonderfully complex! Your workmanship is marvelous—how well I know it."*

Once you are able to look at yourself as a child of God, his beautiful unique creation, you can begin to love yourself. Now you can embrace the person that your Creator intended you to be. He gave you those likes and dislikes. He gave you your personality. He made you with a purpose and a plan; a purpose and a plan to serve him, to bring him pleasure.

I know that reading your Bible and praying daily may sound cliché or "churchy", but it is vital to a healthy relationship with

Christ. The Bible is God's Word to his followers. He will open your mind to understanding if you embrace and meditate on his word. If your only source of the Bible is listening to your pastor on Sunday mornings, how can you expect to thrive in your Christian walk? Also, you should never just simply take a teacher at his word. It is vital that you study and know the Bible so you can guard yourself against false teachers. Instead of you saying, "Well Pastor So and So said, such and such", wouldn't *you* rather know what God's word has to say?

Daily structured prayer is also vital. I talk to God almost constantly all throughout my day. But when I slow things down, when I find a quiet private place and go to him in prayer; that is where I discover growth and encouragement.

Meditation is also very important. Meditation is simply prayer, however when you meditate, you are quieting the mind. You sit very quietly, focus on your breathing, and clear your mind. Breathe in through your nose the newness and good that is God. Breathe out through your mouth, "The Old Man", Allow God to speak to you at this time.

There are several good books on the market that teach meditation skills, and I highly recommend reading one of them.

Be a student of life. Always be learning, always be teachable. Read books, listen to music that opens your mind and your spirit to what God wants to teach you. Always be aware of the people that you surround yourself with. Avoid time spent with those individuals that will drag you down and pull you away from your relationship with Christ. I call these people sponges, and I've learned to avoid spending large amounts of time with these people. Likewise, try to surround yourself with people who encourage you, people who help draw you toward Christ, not away from him.

As a Christ Follower, we all need accountability. Pray for, and seek out a mentor in your life. Someone who has walked many years with God and has a healthy, stable Christ—walk. Someone who has the time and is willing to invest in you.

It was discussed at the beginning of this book... many of us, sadly, have been "cut and bruised" deeply by The Christian Church. If this is a struggle for you, this must be addressed. The Bible is very clear about the importance of believers coming together in order to worship God and to hear His Word taught to us. Not to mention all of the ministry opportunities provided at a healthy vibrant church. The first step is simply finding a church to attend. We must understand this simple fact; people are people. Sometimes we are mean, stupid, idiots! We do hurt each other. We say things that we should never say, we ignore people who need loved. I'm simply saying, do not let other people get in your way of being a follower of The Christ. So often when I'm hurt by someone, if I'm truly honest about it, the primary reason my feelings were hurt was due to my sinful pride. The bottom line, if you are going to follow Christ, you cannot be solo; you need a church family, not only for your own growth and support, but to learn to love and serve others.

You've probably heard the saying, "this ain't no dress rehearsal". Embrace this life that you've been given. Seek The Christ out with your entire being, and stop allowing the enemy to creep into your life bringing self-destruction and havoc. The beauty of eternity is well beyond human comprehension. This life is preparing us for eternity, you are an eternal creature. Now begin living your life with an eternal perspective.

FLORIDA

I've dreamt of the ocean most of my adult life. I've imagined the scent of the salt air breathed into my nostrils, the hot salty air whirling around my face. The warmth of the coastal sun giving new life to this land-locked Ohio boy. I could only imagine what it would feel like to plunge into the salty ocean water, to feel the power of the ocean grabbing hold of me. The sheer vastness of the ocean, I find simply beyond comprehension. I've always imagined the ocean being a spiritual experience.

One of the closest friends that I have ever had, owns a home in Florida, on the Florida East Coast. So now, there was a specific place for me to envision in my mind's eye. A community that I could live in. A community by the ocean. A dream, a vision of a future life. A life filled with walks on the beach, a life of swimming in the ocean. A new life without ice and snow.

Well, finally an opportunity was coming to life! My friend invited me and my beautiful bride to come stay at his place for our vacation. Needless to say, we took him up on the offer!

We loaded up the car and headed eighteen hours south.

Now my wife and I are true soul mates. We are a couple of cracked nuts that just simply belong together. Other than falling madly in love with each other, and being madly in love with *us*, we got married because we really enjoy doing life together. So an eighteen hour road trip to Florida was just the thing for us.

The drive down was fun and uneventful. We pulled into our friends driveway exhausted from the long drive.

The next morning, I sprang out of bed like a little boy on Christmas morning. Our host had breakfast cooking… the aroma was mouthwatering.

After a delicious breakfast, and three cups of life-giving coffee, we were packing coolers, grabbing towels and chairs… and off to the beach we went!

My heart was pounding. At the age of forty-four, I was finally going to fully experience the ocean. Would it be all that

I had imagined that it would be? Would I love it the way that I thought and hoped that I would?

Our host parked his van. He, Tina, and I hopped out and unloaded the beach stuff, and away we marched, our fearless leader showing the way. We walked up the wooden steps to the wooden trail that lead to the beach. There it was, in all of its glory... Not just the beach, but that vast, mysterious ocean. The air smelled amazing. Everyone we walked past was smiling. It was as if the beach was a giant happy pill! Tina and I were smiling very big as well.

The leader of this motley trio, staked out our spot. It was obvious that he was a regular beach goer. I watched him and followed his lead, trying not to look like a tourist.

After sitting in my chair for a while soaking up the warm rays from the sun, I simply couldn't stand it any longer! I had to *experience* the ocean. I looked over at my beautiful bride, "Hey Baby, you want to go check out the water?" She looked over at me with those amazing brown eyes, and her crooked little grin, "Sure, sounds great". She had that look on her face, like she was waiting for me to ask, you know, the way ladies do that sort of thing.

We hopped up, grabbed hands and headed for the water. We walked slowly into the ocean water. We were both laughing like little kids. The more we laughed, the less sure-footed we became. I can only imagine what we must have looked like to anyone that may have been watching us.

So on we went. The waves were pretty good that day. Further out I went. My bride stayed behind, cheering me on, both of us laughing the entire time like a couple of young kids. I moved farther out, the water was up to my stomach and chest area. It was amazing. It was exhilarating. However, the true rush hadn't yet come.

I was up to my chest in the warm ocean water, I turned from the beach to face the endless ocean. "HOLY CRAP!" what seemed like a very large wave was headed straight at me! I really didn't know how I was supposed to navigate this wave. Fortunately for me, my instincts kicked in and I simply let myself go. The wave swallowed me up whole! As quickly as it had swallowed me up, it gently spit me back out. I came up out of the water hooping and woohooing, and laughing like a seven-year-old school boy. I stood to my feet to try to take in what had just occurred, but before I could even think—BAM! Another small, but powerful wave hit me from behind, knocking me off of my feet. I got up again, this time making more ruckus than the time before. My wife and I were laughing so hard that we both had difficulty breathing.

After I got my wits about myself, I turned around and stared at the ocean. This vast, endless body of water. So much power. So much might. Just one small expression of my Creator, God Almighty.

This is the moment when it happened. Standing there at that moment, taking all of this in… something down deep within my soul awoke. Something that I did not know I held within. This was an incredible spiritual experience. It's as though my soul had been quietly crying out for the ocean. This part of me was drinking it all in; coming to life. I somehow felt more alive at that moment than I've ever felt in my entire life. To complete this perfect moment, behind me I heard the soothing laughter of my Soul Mate. I turned to look at her, and there she was knee deep in the ocean, giggling and playing in the water. Our eyes met, we both laughed… a perfect moment that I shall treasure for the rest of my life.

Psalms 68:34 (NLT) *"Tell everyone about God's power. His majesty shines down on Israel; his strength is mighty in the heavens.*

1 Samuel 2:2 (NLT) *"No one is holy like the Lord! There is no one besides you; there is no Rock like our God.*

Romans 1:20 (NLT) *"For ever since the world was created, people have seen the earth and sky. Through everything God made, they can clearly see his invisible qualities—his eternal power and divine nature. So they have no excuse for not knowing God."*

PURGED

I stepped into the ocean today
The waves,
They are as the voice of God
I discern them
As their roar whispers to me
The world is left behind
My mind is quieted
Only the immense roar
Do I hear.
This roar heals,
It soothes my broken, fragmented mind.
I am silenced.
Silenced as He speaks,
As He heals.
Time has become vapor,
The scurry washed away
Cleansed
I am nothing in this vastness
The salt air cleanses…
I am purged.

Psalms 51:7 (NLT) *"Purify me from my sins, and I will be clean; wash me, and I will be whiter than snow.*

2 Timothy 2:21 (NLT) *"If you keep yourself pure, you will be a special utensil for honorable use. Your life will be clean, and you will be ready for the Master to use you for every good work."*

John 15:2 (NLT) *"He cuts off every branch of mine that doesn't produce fruit, and he prunes the branches that do bear fruit so they will produce even more."*

Jeremiah 17:10 (NLT) *"But I, the Lord, search all hearts and examine secret motives. I give all people their due rewards, according to what their actions deserve."*

SPIRITUAL FUSION ASSESSMENT

Okay, it is now time to get out your journal and reflect. It is time to be brutally honest with yourself.

1. Does the thought of sharing your faith with others frighten you? If so, why do you think that is?
2. In a world where purity is something that is mocked, do you seek out a life of purity?
3. Take a moment to look at your current life. Is your life bearing healthy fruit?
4. Are you physically, literally where you want to be?

You only have this one life here on earth. Do not live it in regret. Do not live in shame. Stop walking to the beat of this world. God has offered you his grace, and has given you your own individual "beat".... So start marching in Spiritual Fusion with your Creator, and leave the Old Man behind.

ACKNOWLEDGEMENTS

∞Thank you infinity∞

Tina, my bride. I think of the endless hours that you poured into this project, assisting me and supporting me. No words do justice. I love you and thank God every day for you.

Pat Harless, we have laughed until we cried, we have cried until we laughed. Thank you for partaking in the conversations that most will not. You have challenged me. You have sharpened me. You never give up on me.

James Harless, where do I begin? What do I say? I love you Bro. (Please at least acknowledge that Robot Heaven is conceivable).

Jane Carroll, your hours spent editing. Your feedback was priceless.

Dad, what can I say? Your wisdom, your love, your humility, and mostly your support….

Jim Hanf, it was a thrill watching you break the box.

Greg Pfal, you and that boyish spirit. Never stop being you brother.

Marty McCabe, we are so different from each other. Thanks for the youth ministry days.

Dan Glover, mentor of men.

Bill Lyle, preaching Christ fearlessly.

ABOUT THE AUTHOR

Timothy W. Carroll began writing prose and poetry during his early teenage years. Timothy's writings began as something very private and very personal. It was a form of journaling for him.

From a very early age Timothy secretly began to suffer from serious bouts of anxiety and depression; emotions that he simply did not understand. He discovered early on that reading and writing were a healthy escape from these up and down, unexplained emotions.

As Timothy reached his mid-teens, his secret battle with anxiety and depression only deepened. Like so many people, he began masking those negative feelings with getting high, drunk and engaging in other negative behaviors.

Thus, the nomadic journey that *is* NOMAD began.

Today, Timothy lives in Sunny Florida with his wife, Tina. They have six adult children and enjoy being grandparents to several grandchildren.

Timothy continues to seek out his life passion: To teach others how to avoid the unhealthy nomad life. And to teach those who have found themselves trapped in that solitary place, how to find new hope and meaning for their lives, through Christ.

CONNECT WITH THE AUTHOR

timothywcarroll@gmail.com
http://timothywcarroll.wixsite.com/nomad

HAVE TIMOTHY COME SPEAK TO YOUR GROUP

Church Events, Men's Retreats, Youth Groups, Prison Ministry, Faith-Based Rehabilitation Groups....